National Identity
&
Heritage of India

DR. PRADIP K. BARAT

STAR PUBLISHING

CANADA

Library and Archives Canada Cataloguing in Publication

CIP data on file with the National Library and Archives

ISBN 978-1-926582-63-4

Star Publishing
starpublishing@rogers.com

DEDICATED

to the memory of my parents,

who personified the Vedic life style.

Awake, O my mind,
On the sacred shores of *Bharat**,
the great ocean of Humanity.
Standing here with outstretched arms,
I send my salutations to the God of Humanity,
And in solemn chant sing His praises.
At whose call no one knows,
Came flowing streams of people
And merged into *Bharat**.
The Aryan, the Non-Aryan, the Dravids and Mongols,
The Shakas, Huns, Pathans, and the Moghuls,
Have all merged into one body...

Rabindranath Tagore

This passage is a part of a Bengali poem from *Gitanjali*,
created by Rabindranath Tagore in 1911. He was awarded
the Nobel Prize for this work in 1913. This poem was
translated in 1955 by Aurobindo Bose, a student and protégé
of Rabindranath Tagore.

**Bharat* is the ancient and original Sanskrit name for India.

ACKNOWLEDGEMENTS

I am indebted to my friend Shelagh Harris of
Richmond Hill, Ontario, for her help in editing
this book. I am thankful to my friends
and colleagues Dave Feinstein and Dave Robinson
from York region, Ontario, Canada, for their
advice and encouragement in completing this book.
I am also thankful to Indian music teacher
Deepankar Ganguly of Mississauga, Ontario and
author Frank Robinson of Albany, New York for
their guidance.

PREFACE

This book came about as a collection of my presentations as a guest speaker or lecturer in various high school and undergraduate classes in Canada and the US. Many of these courses contained a component about India. There was a broad range of follow up questions on various topics from students to which this book will respond. These topics are addressed in a categorical and chronological manner. This book can be used as a supplementary source of information for humanities and cultural studies courses.

In establishing a national identity of India, it explores the possibility that, in spite immense diversity, there is some underlying unity in India for a national identity to be formed. Further, it chronicles the foundation and development of the national heritage of India through historical eras and episodes. Finally, some significant social and cultural institutions of India's heritage are described.

India has been a topic of interest for a long time. Its rich culture, social customs, as well as remarkable history have been topics of wonder and appreciation for many scholars. There is a renewed interest and awareness about India in the world as it gains importance as a commercial and economic power. Further, the ever growing Indian Diaspora may like to know more about their ancestral heritage.

This book explores the features, issues, incidents and personalities that have affected formation and development of Indian national identity and heritage. Only the historical facts and issues with profound effect on Indian heritage have been covered.

While studying these issues, some remarkable features have been identified. There is a thread of unity in spite of all diversities that establishes a national identity of India. The foundation of Indian national identity is based on a definite lifestyle. This lifestyle has further nurtured and preserved India's heritage. India's heritage has not only survived during long political domination by foreign powers, it has further prospered and enriched. Also, India's heritage is not something of the past, but is still reflected in daily lives of Indians, and it can be claimed that "India's Past is Present".

In describing the culture of India, scholars have used terms 'Indic', 'Aryan', 'Vedic', 'Shastric', 'Hindu', or 'Indian'. Although these terms do differ in nuances, they have been used to convey the same concept, which has been unaltered in this book when statements of other scholars have been quoted.

A word processor produced in the US has been used to produce this book, and therefore the spellings are in the American format, which, according to the Oxford Dictionary, are acceptable in the 'English' style as well. Keeping in mind that most readers would not have much knowledge of Sanskrit, use of original Sanskrit words has been kept to a minimum.

TABLE OF CONTENTS

PART I – National Identity of India
    Chapter I   Introduction   13
    Chapter II   National Identity of India   17
    Chapter III   Vedic Lifestyle   23

PART II – Foundation of Indian Heritage
    Chapter IV   India's Physical Features   31
    Chapter V   Historical Periods and Sources 35
    Chapter VI   Ancient Civilizations   39

PART III - Development of Indian Heritage
    Chapter VII   Invasions and Settlements   45
    ChapterVIII   Early Kingdoms and Dynasties 50
    Chapter IX   Small Kingdoms   54

PART IV - Indian Heritage through Occupation
    Chapter X   Turkish Incursions   61
    Chapter XI   Moghul Occupation   66
    Chapter XII   British Colonization   71

PART V - Indian Heritage through Resistance
    ChapterXIII   Maratha Resurgence   81
    Chapter XIV   Sikh Resistance   85
    Chapter XV   Revolts and Rebellion   89

PART VI - Indian Heritage in Modern Age
    Chapter XVI   Renaissance and Reformation 97
    Chapter XVII   Rise of Nationalism   103
    Chapter XVIII   Struggle for Self-Rule   108

PART VII - Indian Heritage in Independent India
    Chapter XIX   Mass Movement   115
    Chapter XX   Partition and Independence   120
    Chapter XXI   Nehru-Gandhi "Dynasty"   125
    Chapter XXII   Rise of Regionalism   130

PART VIII – Indian Heritage: Cultural Institutions
    Chapter XXIII   Dharma: A Way of Life   137
    Chapter XXIV   Philosophy   142
    Chapter XXIV   Sanskrit   148
    Chapter XXVI   Science & Mathematics   153
    Chapter XXVII   Music and Dance   161
    Chapter XXVIII   Arts and Architecture   169

PART IX - Summary and Conclusion   179

Chapter References   187
References   197
Front Cover   201

PART I

NATIONAL IDENTITY OF INDIA

Chapter I
INTRODUCTION

There is an anecdote about an American informing his Indian friend that he is going to India. The Indian friend enquires, "Which one?" The implication is that Indian society is far too diverse for one to fully experience. Therefore, it is rather difficult to establish a comprehensive and universally accepted notion of national identity for India.

It is easy to misunderstand India, particularly for individuals with a sense of linear thinking based on empirical evidence. History shows that, in the West, 'civilization' is an amalgam of materialism, technology and military power, in India they are not. In the West, most development to 'civilization' took place top down, mainly from feudalism, stimulated by renaissance, and then led by benevolent rulers, particularly during the Age of Enlightenment, and then benefiting from industrial revolution. In India, 'civilization' mainly developed through thinkers and reformers, sages and seers from common populace, who had no official status or military power. Being colonized, India has missed the industrialization and introduction of social welfare system phases of development as well. The West has well documented history; India has myths and legends, and unwritten knowledge transmitted by oral tradition.

Unlike the West, the civilization in India developed not in cities surrounded by walls, but in serene, peaceful and natural surroundings, known as "aranya" or woods, through contemplation and meditation, manifested in spiritual, philosophical, literary and artistic concepts. As Indian poet Rabindranath Tagore wrote in his book '*Tapovan*':

"Contemporary western civilization is built of brick and wood. It is rooted in the city. But Indian civilization has been distinctive in locating its source of regeneration, material and intellectual, in the forest, not in city. India's best ideas have come where man was with communication with trees and rivers and lakes, away from the crowds. The peace of the forest has helped the intellectual evolution of man"

The most often repeated description of India is "diverse". The Government of India's website, *"National Portal of India"* uses the phrase "unity in diversity". Many other words and phrases have been used to describe India. Al Beruni, an Arab scholar who visited India around 1000 CE, has described India as having "great philosophers, good scientists and mathematicians"[5], and the British considered India as a "jewel in the crown" of the British Empire. Many British authors, such as, Jim Corbett, H.G.Wells and Rudyard Kipling, have described India as "enchanting", "romantic", "mysterious", "spiritual" and "mystical". In the twentieth century, before the economic improvement, India has been described as poverty-stricken, disaster-prone, teeming with hungry masses, and difficult to govern.

Even the name for the country India is controversial and diverse. Some fundamentalists prefer to call it "Aryavarta" or the abode of the Aryans to stress the influence and importance of Aryan civilization. Many communal leaders, such as Muhammad Ali Jinnah, the founder and first Governor General of Pakistan, called it "Hindustan" or the land of the Hindus. Jawahar Lal Nehru, the first Prime Minister of Independent India, declared the official name as "India", invoking the origin of Indus Valley civilization. Jinnah complained that since the entire Indus Valley is in present Pakistan, Nehru had no right to refer to the rest as India. The Hindi term for India is "Bharat", named after a legendary ruler according to the epic '*Mahabharata*'. Modern day Indian sociologists like to describe the two economic and social segments as India and Bharat: India composed of educated, middle class people, whereas, Bharat consisting of under-educated and conservative people, belonging to the poor class.

As the economic conditions in India improve due to business opportunities for Indian entrepreneurs, mainly in the Information Technology and Biochemistry sectors, India is now considered to be on the verge of becoming an "economic superpower".

Like many other societies, India has some of the features of India's identity are acquired and mutable, while others are inherited and constant[2]. India has a multicultural society composed of diverse people migrating, settling and establishing new communities. Indian society is extremely dynamic, adjusting and adapting to historical upheavals, experimenting and assimilating social and cultural changes, while maintaining its original way of life and emerging as a renewed but vigorous society[1].

In modern India, old ways retain their influence, effectiveness and strong presence, but new ways are also making inroads in political, social and cultural areas as well. While changing due to both external influence and internal evolutions, and with little resistance and conflict, India has maintained and preserved much of its ancient way of life.

When most nations are desperately trying to adjust to multiculturism in a globalized world, India has been building powerful and vibrant social institutions of cultural assimilation throughout her existence. India "has emerged as a world region in modern times, because a particular constellation of social identities has become essential for people living there through the operation of powerful social institutions"[3]. The most integral layer of Indian existence, to many scholars, is the solid foundation of social institutions. India's geographical boundaries have changed many times over the centuries. Ruling dynasties have flourished and floundered, the economy has gone through many periods of upheavals, through it all, the social, cultural and religious aspects of Indian society, thanks to a robust foundation, have remained upbeat and strong. One can argue that they have emerged more vigorous and powerful from those challenges.

To understand India and its identity, one must explore this country's unique capability to renew itself. India's society and its cultural institutions have survived dogmatic missionaries, numerous invasions, migrations and settlements, and close to thousand years' long occupation and colonization by foreign powers. Social customs and cultural activities have not only remained a strong foundation of Indian society, they have been enriched and strengthened by from these experiences.

Any truism or summarizing statement about India can be easily contradicted. There is no 'one way' for any aspect of India. In spite of all the contradictions and diversities, one can find a foundation of profound religiosity and spirituality, within an established paradigm of inclusiveness and flexibility. "...India has been rather like traditional Indian music: the broad basic rules are firmly set, but within that, one is free to improvise, unshackled by a written score"[8].

The staggering, often striking contrasts in India are both frustrating and confusing. Here, history and traditions are strongly held, which coexists with accepting and assimilating features. India preserved its link with the past which remains as ever present[7]. Yet it has embraced a democratic tradition, with an education system rivaling the West, and introducing technological advancements with relative ease.

Here, the factors necessary to establish a coherent form of a national identity will be defined and elaborated. It will further explore significant social and cultural institutional traits that are based on these factors. The validity of the theory that, unlike most nations, India's national identity is a product of social and cultural institutions and practices, based on an ancient way of life will be exlpored. With a tendency to live with contradictions and plurality without conflicts, the identity is not an entity formed by a political establishment, or racial and ethnic traits of its people. These institutions are unique in nature, as they accepted the various cultures of invading and settling groups without losing their originality. As a result, these institutions have turned into India's national heritage.

In the process of exploring India's national identity, it is essential to study the geographical features and historical episodes of India, as "Our times and our thoughts are largely shaped by the past. That shaping is one reason we study history",[6] . Further, "History provides much of the fuel of nationalism. It creates collective memories that help to bring the nation into being...To study the past may help us understand better how we came to be who we are..."[5]. Historian Eric Hobsbawn has stressed that "nationalism is modern but it invents itself history and traditions". The study of geographical feature of a nation is necessary because "Geography is the matrix of history",[1].

This book will then describe the process of founding, developing and enriching factors of India's national heritage, which are influenced by India's physical features and historical periods. Finally, some social and cultural institutions of India's heritage will be described.

Chapter II
National Identity of India

To establish national identity, it is imperative to set the definitions of both individual identity and a nation, and only then, the definition of the national identity of a nation can be formulated. Individual identity has been defined as, "Gender, ethnicity, sexual preference, age, class, nationality, religion, family, clan, geography, occupation, and, of course, history can go into ways that we define our identity".[10]

Etymologically, the word "nation" is derived from the Latin root "natio", which, depending on context, means: being born, a race, or a set of people[8]. These concepts are somewhat incomplete to define a nation, and further attributes for a nation are necessary. According to *The Dictionary of History of Ideas*, some of these attributes are, "having a common descent, a common language, a common culture, a common religion"[17].

Most nations are composed of inhabitants with a common culture often the result of assimilation to or domination of the culture of the ruling class or the majority. Language is one of these features that unite a nation, and the lack of a common language often results in separatist movements, such as in Canada and Belgium. However, "Most modern nations are the product of a fusion of population groups over the centuries, to the point where one element is indistinguishable from the next".[17] Historian Theodore Herzel summed it as, "A nation is a historical group of men of recognizable cohesion, held together by a common enemy". All these factors contribute to a sense of national identity- both by uniting the people of the nation and also by distinguishing them from other such groups.

An important characteristic of national identity is a common descent. People from common descent tend to display enough commonalities which can emerge as a basis of national identity. For example, people from Europe have imposed their identities and heritage on the aboriginal people of South and North America. A common language among the inhabitants can be a basis of a national identity. Many nations, such as, France, Spain, Italy and Germany in Europe, Iran in the Middle East, Pakistan and Japan in Asia, have specific and distinct languages as their national identities. Some nations also develop a common culture, and it is nurtured and carried on by later generations. In this process, the common culture becomes a basis of a national identity.

Gellner claims that "National identity refers both to the distinguishing features of a group, and to the individuals' sense of belonging to it"[4]. This process of establishing a national identity can be used to search for a national identity of India. Considering the complex and diverse features of India, and often the conflicting and contradictory forces at work at the ethnic, linguistic and religious levels, it is just as difficult to establish an acceptable framework to define a national identity.

In some cases, a distinct geographical feature may become the basis of nation formation. A landmass surrounded by water, such as, Australia and Japan are some such examples. Albania has become a nation while being surrounded by mountains. India is surrounded by the Himalayan mountain range in the north, and by the Indian Ocean in the south.

Diversity in India is overwhelming. According to an informative portal created in 2008 by the Government of India, there are over one billion people, six major ethnic groups, twenty-eight states organized on linguistic and ethnic basis, there are twenty two official and thirty-three spoken languages and over two thousand dialects with eleven distinct scripts, and nine main world religions in India. India also has diverse climates, geographical varieties and landforms, resulting in more diversity in food habits, dwelling types, social customs and cultural activities. "If caste and language complicate the notion of Indian identity, ethnicity makes it more difficult", [15].

Remarkably, contradictions can be found in almost all sectors of Indian lives, proving the statement: Any tautology about India can be immediately contradicted. Examples of lifestyles spanning several centuries can be found in India. The streets are shared by a wide spectrum of vehicles: from cars, horse and buggies, auto rickshaw to the latest luxury cars. People wearing ancient form of Dhotis and Saris do walk by people wearing Muslim styled Salwar or Jodhpurs, as well as Western styled suits and skirts, T-shirts and blue jeans

Steps away from glittering shopping malls selling internationally known brand name and designer products, one can find street vendors selling fish and chicken, cosmetics and clothing, household products and spices, just as they did in ancient times. In most construction sites, scores of women carry bricks and stone chips on their heads, climbing up bamboo scaffolding, right beside mighty cranes and huge earth-moving machinery.

Although there are hundreds of world class educational institutions, only sixty-one percent of the total population of India is literate. One can find highly skilled scientists and engineers, trained with analytical and logical skills, consulting astrological charts to plan important activities, both in personal and professional lives. In addition to a modern, internationally recognized health care system, several alternate systems are also found, such as the ancient Indian system of Ayurveda, as well as Homeopathic, Hakimi, Yuani, and even a number of faith healing systems. The Government of India has created a website to provide information for these alternate health care systems "To provide scientific industrial R&D that maximizes the economic, environmental and societal benefits for the people of India" (www.tkdl.res.in).

All of these diversities and contradictions pale when compared to economic disparity. The gulf between the "haves" and "have-nots" has been growing, particularly after the economic boom harnessed by trained professionals and businessmen in the field of science and technology. This boom has expanded the middle class, and raised the lifestyle of millions. However, millions still live under the poverty line. Mumbai, which is the financial and commercial capital of India, and home to wealthy and glamorous Bollywood celebrities and many millionaires, also has the largest slum "Dharavi", with over one million slum dwellers living in an area less than half of the size of Central Park in New York.

India has a long and complicated history with several dynasties, full with peaceful and prosperous eras punctuated by invasions, intrigues, revolts, rebellions, battles and wars. Politically, India is relatively a new entity. During the last five thousand years of known history, over fifty percent of this land has been ruled by a single ruler for only a short period of three hundred years. Before independence, no ruler or dynasty ever ruled the whole of India. Even during the British rule, there were over three hundred princely states, with a varying degree of internal administrative rights vested on the Indian rulers, but strictly controlled by a 'resident' or a representative of the British Government in India [6].

Considering the diversities, some scholars claim that there is no cohesiveness in India to form a national identity. According to some historians, this land possesses "not a singular history, but rather many histories, with indefinite, contested origins... and (Indian) history's multiplicity, antiquity and ambiguity have become more complicated"[9]. Some sociologists claim that these diversities have developed strong passions for regionalism and ethnocentricity, and thus have "failed to construct the nation of India",[1].

A closer study of the life style of Indians reveals that there is a unique lifestyle based on ancient values and attributes that transcends all diversities. These values and attributes originated during the Vedic ages around 2000 BC, and spread with the rise of Aryan civilizations[3]. Some such attributes include: a belief in strong family bonds, acknowledgement of the community, social and cultural values, practice of 'Ahimsa' or non-violence, respect for elders, quest for knowledge, appreciation of nature, believing in the eventuality as a result of own's actions or Karma, accepting a life based on spirituality, and recognizing the divine existence in all aspects of life. These attributes have been chronicled by Sage Manu in *Manu Smriti* (Chapter 6, Stanza 92), which has been further elaborated in later chapters.

India's geography and history have also provided some remarkable factors of unity. As the region is nestled between the difficult to cross Himalayan-mountain- range and the Indian Ocean, the inhabitants had to rely on each other. Most invaders and settlers also remained in India and were integrated while preserving their uniqueness. Several great rulers in different dynasties, such as Chandragupta Maurya, Chandragupta Vikramaditya, Asoka and Akbar have provided unified and peaceful periods, resulting in more structure for unity. The cultural aspects of Indian life, developed among the masses, and not necessarily under the patronage of the rulers, remained immune to political turmoil. Diversity and continuity are the most striking features of India, as it is isolated by the mighty mountain chain of the Himalayas from the rest of Asia in the north, and surrounded by the Indian Ocean in the south.

Due to this geographical isolation, the cultural aspects of India, such as, philosophy and literature, science and mathematics, arts and architecture, music and dance, not only survived in spite of such diversities, but prospered during all the upheavals of history. India has a unique way of compromising and accepting contradictions. The ability to cope with diversity has been achieved through compartmentalization. Diversity has not only been tolerated and accepted in India, it has been celebrated and preserved. Foreign cultures have enriched the original culture, and thus become a part of Indian culture. Indians have accepted Muslim culinary, fashion habits, and adapted Western styles of work at the professional and business levels, while maintaining enriched personal lives immersed in traditional values based on ancient norms and attributes.

Much of India's literature and arts reflects the philosophical and cultural basis developed in ancient times, and cherished throughout India. The epics of *Ramayana* and *Mahabharata*, which have been translated in almost all major Indian languages, are understood and celebrated all over India. Yoga and meditation are practiced by individuals from all sections and regions. Vedas are respected and venerated, and Sanskrit is recognized and revered as a sacred language, in addition of being the origin of most Indian languages. Throughout the ages, many religious and social reformers, such as Kabir and Nanak, Ramakrishna and Vivekananda, Nazrul and Gandhi, have all called for religious harmony and unity. Festivals and rituals representing all world religions are celebrated in India.

Emphasizing this point, it has been pointed out that, "The whole idea of Indianess is its pluralism", and "The idea of India is of one land embracing many. It is the idea that a nation may endure differences of caste, creed, color, conviction, culture, cuisine, costume, and custom, and still rally around a consensus"[15]. To stress this point, Tharoor, a former Undersecretary General of United Nations, describes one aspect of the "Bangladesh War" between India and Pakistan: It was ordered by a Hindu Prime Minister (India Gandhi), commanded by a Zoroastrian (Marshall Manekshaw), under the air protection provided by a Moslem (Air Commander Lateef), led by a Sikh (Lieutenant General Arora), and the surrender of Pakistani forces was supervised by a Jew (Major General Jacobs).

Other than culture and religion, two topics of great passion in India have ushered in more unity; they are Bollywood movies and the game of Cricket. Bollywood personalities, as well as all cricket players, represent all religions, ethnicities, languages and regions. Fans do not care about their backgrounds, consider them heroes, and adore their talents.

Other scholars have noted that the unifying foundation for India is based on spirituality and religiosity. "India today is a land of single culture, and one of the strongholds of traditional Hinduism. The fundamental unity of India is a cultural and not a racial phenomenon", [13]. This foundation is not a religious dogma based on a specific doctrine, but a set of values for understanding the essence of life, realizing the importance of knowledge and appreciating music, arts and dance, in short, a way of life.

The unity of India has been stated to be built on a foundation of culture and civilization. "Indians, beyond all doubt, possess a deep underlying fundamental unity, far more than that produced, either by geographical isolation or by political suzerainty. That unity transcends the innumerable diversities of blood, color, language, dress, manners and sect" and "The essential Indian Unity rests upon the fact that the diverse peoples of India have developed a peculiar type of culture and civilization, utterly different from any other type in the world; that civilization may be summed up in the term of 'Hinduism'"[12]. Further, "India, like Europe, is held together by a shared set of basic religious and cultural assumptions, beliefs, values, and practices",[16]. Finally, "More than any country in the world, India's culture and society has been molded by religion. Even today, it remains the single most important influence in Indian life",[14].

This unifying idea has been described by scholars as 'Hindu' by Robb (2002), 'Indic' by Aloysius (1997), 'Aryan' by Wood (2007), and 'Vedic' by Embree (1958), which can be regarded as a catalyst for Indian National Identity. "Indian nationalism is the nationalism of an idea, the idea of an ever-ever land, emerging from an ancient civilization, united by shared history, sustained by pluralist democracy",[18]. To avoid any religious, geographical, or racial bias, the term "Vedic" way of life will be used to explore this form of unifying foundation to establish India's National identity.

Chapter III
VEDIC LIFE STYLE

The foundation of Vedic life style was affirmed in the numerous maxims and adages, and based on literary and song form in the *Vedas*, later elaborated in the *Upanishads, Puranas*, and the epics *Ramayana* and *Mahabharata*. The Vedic life style developed during Vedic civilization, which is perhaps the earliest documented Indian civilization, originating between 2500 BCE and 2000 BCE, and known as the Vedic period[2]. It is so termed as most of the information about this era is found in *Rig Veda*, the earliest one of four scriptures, called Vedas, or Books of Knowledge. Other three Vedas are *Sama, Yayur*, and *Atharva*. Vedas literally mean "Books of Knowledge". "The Vedas are the most important source of information about the Vedic Aryans and the same time the greatest cultural achievement",[3].

Towards the end of 600 BCE, a score of texts known as Upanishads, or *Vedanta*, meaning 'end of Vedas' were attached to the Vedas. The Upanishads presented explanations and interpretations of Vedas, and were the foundations of philosophical treaties. "The Upanishads cannot be regarded as presenting a consistent, homogeneous, or unified philosophical system, though there are certain doctrines held in common. Divergences of method, opinion, and conclusion are everywhere apparent even within a single Upanishad",[2]. These doctrines became the very foundation of all values and customs found in Indian culture. As time progressed, more scriptures, called *Srutis, Smritis* and *Puranas*, were prepared by '*Sadhus*' or Sages. *Manu Smriti*, so named as it was prepared by Manu, who set and explained a code of conduct for all in Vedic society. Although officially secular, much of Indian constitution and laws have significant traces of the Laws of Manu.

These scriptures, originally compiled orally, describe the Vedic life as it was during the Vedic era. The norms stated in these scriptures were not set by royal proclamations or commanded through divine revelation. Vedic life style was popularized and internalized both by the learned and illiterate, nobles and commoners. Original ideas, stated in classical Sanskrit, are often difficult to translate into modern languages. The ideas contain theoretical ideals rich with the philosophical and spiritual themes, and also describe means to practise such ideals.

Codes of conduct have been described in '*Smritis*', which are explanations of Vedas as chronicled by scholars. One of them, as mentioned before, is '*Manusmriti*' written by the ancient sage Manu, which prescribes 10 essential aspects of Dharma (Chapter 6, Stanza 92): patience (*dhriti*), forgiveness (*kshama*), piety or self control (*dama*), purity (*shauch*), control of senses (*indraiya-nigrah*), reason (*dhi*), knowledge or learning (*vidya*), truthfulness (*satya*) and absence of anger (a*krodha*).

Early forms of Vedas were only oral; they were composed in poetic form in Sanskrit. Rig Veda contains hymns, ritual texts, and philosophical treaties. It contains rich celebrations of nature and reflections upon creation, life and death in colorful poetic verses. Rig Veda is also regarded as the best source of information on the daily life of the Vedic Aryans, their struggles and aspirations, their religious and philosophical ideas. As further study indicates, much of these features can be found in the daily lives of most Indians at the present time.

Even though the gulf between the ideals stated in the Vedic scriptures and the practices in the modern times might have changed, but the fundamental beliefs and ideals have remained ingrained in thoughts and feelings of most Indians[1]. The fundamental concepts and practices of the Vedic way of life have remained strong, and set the values and customs followed by Indian families and communities. When these values were in conflict with the laws and regulations set by the authorities, the Vedic values usually triumphed, and the rulers' edicts were ignored. This process kept the Vedic ideals alive during the often conflicting laws imposed by the authorities. This was most evident during Muslim occupation and British colonization.

The ideas of indestructible soul as a part of the Divine soul, and the transmigration of soul were introduced in the Upanishads. These ideas resulted in developing the concept of '*Moksa*' or the process of reuniting the soul with the Divine. This concept followed the belief in non-materialism and inevitability of predestined fate. When followed literally to the extreme, as it has been done, these concepts may lead to passivity and resignation, although those have been repudiated in the *Shrimadbhagawat Gita*, a section of the epic *Mahabharata*.

Vedic civilization mostly prospered in small villages, and its surrounding woods were used as places of meditation and contemplation. By the sixth century BCE, agriculture had become the main occupation, and trades of pottery, carpentry and cloth-weaving was beginning to take place. No large cities or even large buildings were built. The dwellings were made of straw, bamboo and mud. The walls of these dwellings were adorned with artistic decorations using rice paste. Vedic settlements were administered by a 'ruler', advised by a council of elders or *'sabhas'* or *'samitis'*, and sanctioned by a priest, called 'purohit' or 'the learned one'[6]. These types of Samitis, at present known as *Panchayats*, have been introduced in modern India, and now they form the basis of local administration in Indian villages.

The foundation of social life during the Vedic age was the family, and all members of the family respected each other and lived in complete cooperation. Extended families tended to settle in one place, and lived off the land, forming a *'Gotra'* or clan. The Gotra and names of ancestors, with the original locality, are still evoked during formal social and religious ceremonies. The extended family gradually broke down into joint families, where several families lived in a single household. This system offered mutual safety and a sense of belonging, but demanded sacrifice from all members of the family. In modern times, the joint family system has practically ceased as most young people move away to their location of employment. In Vedic times the basis of their society was the family, and the society itself was composed of the whole race irrespective of their function or class. Even today, family is regarded as the most important unit of Indian society.

People were grouped into four 'Varnas" or classes, based on their contribution to society and performance of functions. This division of society, based on occupation in the beginning of the Vedic Age, changed into *'Jatis'* or castes, as it is known today. 'Jatis' were endogamous groups representing functional distinctions or occupations within a *'Varna'*. As time went on, new 'Jatis' were formed when members of different 'Varnas' intermingled, or changed their profession, and also when foreign tribes were absorbed in Indian society [7]. "Caste" is a Portuguese term, which is a misnomer in this case, and still today, the implications of Castes are widely misunderstood, particularly outside India.

During the Vedic period, women enjoyed a respected position in family, and they joined their husbands and participated in most religious activities. Women have been mentioned as leaders in society. In later scriptures, or '*Puranas*', heroic triumphs of many female deities over the evils are chronicled, and they are celebrated in many social and religious activities throughout India. Early scriptures, particularly the epics and the Puranas, affirm that both arranged marriages and '*Gandharva*'' marriages or marriage after courtship were practised. According to a survey conducted by the British Broadcasting Corporation in 2008, over sixty percent of all marriages are still arranged in India.

The food was simple but nourishing. As the Aryan civilization thrived on the Ganges, fertile soil and tropical weather presented the inhabitants with an abundant amount and a variety of fruits and grains. In addition to fruits, honey and cow milk products were used abundantly. Perhaps because of their usefulness, cows were deemed not to be slaughtered. Cotton, wool, bark, and leather from deer and tiger were used to make dresses. Dresses were usually wrapped around, and turbans were commonly used, both by males and females. Color was produced from pastes of flower and leaves. Sandalwood pastes were used as cosmetics. This practice is still followed in India today.

For entertainment, dances, songs and instruments such as flutes, drums, and lutes were used. Music and dances were not only social activities, but essential components of religious activities as well. In the epics of '*Ramayana*' and '*Mahabharata*', the art of dancing and singing are prescribed as part of the education. More information about music and dance are found in the text of '*Natyashastra*', chronicled around 200 BCE. The hymns contained in Vedas were chanted rhythmically and recited in songs[3]. Songs and dances are still significant features of religious and social activities in India.

The quest for knowledge was emphasized, and learning was regarded as a religious activity. The first part of one's life was expected to be dedicated to learning through listening to a teacher or 'guru'. Learned men and women were regarded as important individuals, and they were respected and patronized by all, including the rulers. The practice of celibacy, yoga and meditation were expected. Philosophical treaties were developed through discourses among the 'learned' class, and some significant forms of philosophical thoughts became part of Vedic civilization. Learning is still greatly valued in India.

The Vedic religion brought in a set of religious beliefs, which were based on the power of nature. The early hymns of Vedas were poetic homage to the attributes of nature, such as the rising sun, flowing rivers, whispering wind, bountiful forests, blooming trees, and the spacious sky. Some of these attributes became icons of Gods, although they were regarded as the symbolic representations of the universal spirit '*Ishwara*'. Religious activities consisting of rituals of offerings and homage to such icons are practised all over India[5].

It is evident that the Vedic life style is still an important feature of Indian life. Many values and ideals, customs and rituals, originated three thousand years ago, still dictates and influences daily lives of millions of Indians.

PART II
FOUNDATION OF INDIAN HERITAGE

Chapter IV
INDIA'S PHYSICAL FEATURES

India's physical features are products of India's geological forms, and as in many other features, they are diverse and varied. According to the Geological Survey of India conducted in 2007, geological evolution of India began about 4.57 billion years ago, when the Indian Plate broke off the subcontinent Pangaea[2]. The Indian Plate drifted off and eventually collided with the Eurasian Plate, and formed the Indian sub-continent around 50 million years ago. India's geographical forms began to emerge. The Himalayan mountain range formed in the Tertiary period, whereas, the Deccan plate formed from the original plate, remained in the southern part of Indian sub continent, The Indo Gangetic alluvial plain formed by eroding the Himalayas by rivers and monsoon rains. This region has some of the most fertile soil found in the country as new silt is continually laid down by the rivers every year.

There are four distinct physical regions in India: the Himalayan Mountain Range, the Indo-Gangetic Alluvial plains, and the Deccan Plateau, and the coastal areas in the South. The north of India is surrounded by mighty Himalayan Mountain Range, with the Karakoram and Hindukush Mountains in the west, and the difficult to penetrate Arakan Mountain Range in the east, blocking passage to Burma and East Asia. This area also has hills clad with dense jungles, and numerous tributaries forming great rivers. "The waters of Indus River system, one of whose lesser tributaries is the Soam, were to become the cradle of North Indian culture, and, like the alluvial valleys of Punjab and Sind, where silt was borne in their torrents, they are perennial gifts of Himalayan ice and snow",[7].

These geographical zones can be further subdivided into areas each with distinct cultural and linguistic features. The Himalayan area contains the State of Kashmir, Bhutan and Sikkim. The Indo Gangetic Plain can be divided into the Western part with Punjab, Rajasthan, and most of Pakistan. This part endured the wrath of most invaders. The eastern part, or Doab Region, forms the centre of most large kingdoms. The Barmha-putra Valley and watershed area of the Ganges remained isolated, until European explorers arrived over the oceans, instead of the northwest passages as the Turkish-Moghul invaders had used. The Deccan Shield remained insulated by the Vindhyachal and Aravalli Mountain Ranges from Aryan influence from the north, and developed the smaller kingdoms and Dravidian culture in the south.

Thus, the geographical features of India have provided much influence in its historical developments, and the formation of the social, cultural and religious basis of India. India has, "another inheritance from Nature itself-the land and its climate"[1]. However, these physical regions have somehow had a positive effect on the history of India. These divisions have resulted in the formation and development of complex and diverse Indian cultures.

"But if for Europe geography decreed fragmentation, for India it intended in integrity",[3]. These diversities have somehow maintained the fundamental aspects of Vedic or Hindu way of life that has resulted in a basis of unity. "However, behind this diversity, the social and operational aspects of Hinduism, as well as its theology and ideology, did provide a unifying framework of remarkable persistency",[6].

Without the great Himalayan Mountain Range, India would have been reduced to an inhabitable desert. "The Himalayan mountain range, the most prominent feature on the face of the earth, grandly shields the subcontinent from the rest of Asia",[3]. Without the monsoon rain all over India and melting glaciers of the north, India would not have nurturing rivers and fertile land with abundant crops. India, then would not have invited so many invading, migrating, exploring and settling peoples throughout history.

Beyond this mountain range, there is the Tibetan Plateau and Gobi Desert. This mountain range has provided a shelter from invasions from the east and north. "The northern mountains have served as a natural protective wall against both invading armies and Arctic winds",[3]. As a result, long term dynasties were able to offer periods of tranquility for the advancement of philosophy, arts and literature. Only the western part of this mountain range has passes, such as Khyber and Bolan, which became routes for most invaders, migrants and settlers.

The two great river systems, Indus and Ganges with their tributaries, provide fertile plains and useful navigational routes from west to east.

With seasonal monsoon rains, and subtropical conditions, this part produces abundant fruits and grains, rice in the humid east and wheat in semi-arid west. These conditions have invited explorers and settlers, and also established flourishing ruling dynasties. "Indian history begins somewhere on the banks of north India's litany of great rivers-either along the river Indus, or amongst the 'five rivers' which are its tributaries, or in the 'two rivers' region between the Jamuna and Ganga",[3]. Also, "...the Indo-Gangetic region became one of the most densely populated areas in India, and not only was the cradle of Indian civilization but witnessed the rise of India's early great empires",[6]. In the east, the Bramhaputra Valley remained relatively isolated until settlers reached the Arakan mountain ranges, and could not go any further.

The next geographical region contains the Vindhyachal Mountain Ranges separating north and south India and the Deccan Plateau, which forms the bulk of Southern India. With Godavari and Krishna River systems, the southern section is also drenched with monsoon rains. This area has tropical conditions, and grows spices and coconuts, and also provides sea food. The south of the Deccan Plateau contains coastal plains leading to the Indian Ocean. The Indian Ocean had been a gateway to the nations of East Asia for commerce, and the spread of Indian culture to the East Asia. These sea routes later became a useful path for European powers to reach, explore and colonize India. As historian Spears pointed out:

"These physical features have exercised a very important influence upon the destiny of India. In the south and Bengal the tropic conditions have endowed these areas with natural products and made them marts of commerce while limiting the energies and physique of the people. In the north the bracing air has nurtured hardier races, which the rich soil has maintained. It has been the northern races which have tended to aggression and the southern whom we have the longest record of commerce"[5].

Most invaders, migrants, and settlers came from harsh living conditions of Asia Minor, the Arabian Peninsula, Persia, and central Asia. They came through the western passes lured by the tales of a land with great expanses, fertile land, abundance of fruits and crops. Once in, they found they were blocked by the Deccan Plateau, and could only spread to the east, until they were stopped by the Arakan mountain ranges. Such groups settled in the northern part of India, forming racial, ethnic and cultural mixtures[4]. In contrast, the southern part of India remained with little sign of such mixtures. "Invading and settling groups superimposed themselves side by side with existing peoples, instead of replacing them. The racial and social divisions, unlike Europe, coexisted instead of layered in hierarchy of power structure",[5].

Finally, "History and the environment are interdependent and Indian history owes much to an environment which has a highly differentiated structure and which in some ways extremely generous but can also prove to be very hostile and challenging to those who have to cope with it"[5].

Chapter V
HISTORICAL PERIODS AND SOURCES

Dividing Indian history in traditional pre-historic, ancient, early, medieval and modern eras has been found to be unsuitable because in many instances, the ancient ways are still readily practised in India, not only in religious activities, but in many facets of daily life as well. "...the traditions of Sanskrit literature are still sacrosanct, Vedic prayers are still said; televised serialisation of the Sanskrit epics can bring the entire Indian nation to a hushed standstill. The compositions of ancient Aryans are not just history; they are the nearest thing to revelation"[3]. Further, "The resurgence of old tradition throughout Indian history prevents the ready transfer of the Western periodisation of history of India. Ancient, mediaeval and modern history cannot be easily identified in India"[4]. Many historians have adopted another division for Indian history: Hindu, Islamic and British periods. This periodisation has also raised controversies, as historians have noted that the Hindu period was not at all homogeneous in its traditions, and they were not replaced by Islamic or the British rule. Therefore, it has been pointed out that this periodisation is "in terms of predominant political structure and not in terms of the religious or ethnic affiliation of the respective rulers"[4]. Also, some historians object to the fact that a religion-based periodisation for Hindu and Islamic eras should not be followed by the nationality-based period of British rule. In this book, only the issues and features which have affected the heritage of India will be explored.

There are very few available recorded sources for Indian history of ancient time: "Prior to the thirteenth century AD, we possess no historical text of any kind, much less such as detailed narrative as we possess in the case of Greece, Rome or China"[6]. The founders of early states were more interested in developing cultural institutions instead of building palaces and monuments with their names prominently inscribed. The literature too was not chronicled or inscribed, they were not chronologically ordered. The recordings are in poetic forms as epics, therefore facts and fictions are interwoven. Many recordings are also religious in nature, therefore may lack objectivity[5]. The rulers were more interested in founding dynasties instead of recording the facts about their administrations.

This lack of record and absence of the names of individuals who originally created such works have disappointed and frustrated historians. "Scholars have often remarked that during this period India lacked a Western sense of history, as no accurate records of past events were kept. India's cyclical rather than linear concept of time, which was conceived as a vast revolving wheel with cycles of creation, destruction and re-creation, perhaps contributed to an indifference towards historical documentation"[2].

The closest word for "History" in Sanskrit is '*Itihasa*', which literally means 'as it ended'. Another word often used for ancient scriptures is '*Itivritta*' meaning 'as the story ended'. Therefore, these chronicles are full of mythology, narratives, and genealogies. Often, the author put himself inside the narration, and has described the events of the past in present form. Such chronicles are composed in poetic form for easy memorization, and are full of figures of speech and poetic licenses.

Some historical sources are found mainly in sacred literature, such as, *Vedas, Upanishads, Puranas*, and the two epics, *Ramayana and Mahabharata*, of Vedic culture. *Srimad Bhagawat Gita* also known as *Gita*, which originally is a part of Mahabharata, narrates the underlying profound philosophical treaties of Dharma, which became the most revered scripture for millions of Hindus. The '*Manusmriti*' or the 'laws of Manu', composed around 1000 BC, gives a glimpse of rules and customs of that period. *Tripitaks* and *Jataks* of Budhist and *Angas* of Jain religions, composed by Buddhist and Jainist monks, also provide much information about Indian cultural and social systems of India. "Jataka stories, for example, some six hundred in number, deal with the incarnations of Buddha before he attained Buddhahood"[10].

Some historical literature also provides excellent sources of early Indian history. '*Arthashastra*' written by Kautilya of Maurya court describes the Maurya rule, and '*Harsa Charita*' describes the Harsa administration. Buddhist texts are also sources of information as well. Kalidasa, a poet of fifth century, wrote several dramas and revealed much of the social system of that time. Around 800 CE, Sankara, a philosopher who is regarded as a Sage, developed the philosophy of monism, and composed numerous hymns which are still recited today[1]. Around the tenth century, illustrated books with paintings on palm leaves and cloth were created.

Some historical buildings, monuments, and works of art, created during the Maurya and Gupta dynasties have been discovered, and they have provided valuable information. The inscriptions on Pillars of Ashoka, Victory Pillar of Chandra Gupta Vikramaditya, and the Allahabad Pillar of Samudra Gupta yield important historical information. "Then there is architectural and archeological evidence in the shape of temples and sculptures and wall paintings"[10]. In the south, Pallava, Chalukya and Chola dynasties also built many temples with beautiful stone sculptures, some in caves, during the eighth century [4].

Foreign travellers, such as Herodotus and Megasthenese of ancient Greece in the fifth century BCE, wrote extensively about the Nanda administration, and its army. Two travellers from China, Fa-hien in 399-414 CE and Hieun Tsang in 629-645 CE from China, came to study and practice Buddhism and spend many years in India, and both have written extensively about India. Fa-Hien came during the rule of Chandragupta Bikramaditya II, of the Gupta dynasty, regarded by historians as the Golden Age of Indian history, and moved monastery to monastery. Hieun Tsang's work described the conditions of Harsha's kingdom. "The work of these two Chinese monks imparts flesh and blood to the bare bones of dates, dynastic names, and formal inscriptions which are the historian's stock in trade for so much of the early period"[4].

After the conquest and occupation by the Islamic rulers, historical documentation increased, mainly by the patronage of the rulers to make their legacy more permanent. "The picture changed radically with India's Islamic rulers who had a passion for documentation; Mughal emperors, for instance, ordered their every act be recorded, and these annals were then selectively put together to form regal histories"[7.] These rulers built mosques, palaces, monuments and mausoleums with inscriptions of royal edicts, 'fatwas', and Koranic verses. Many such constructions were erected on the ruins of Hindu temples, destroyed under the order of the rulers. Moghul emperor Aurangzeb became well-known for his zeal to destroy much of Hindu scriptures and temples.

Moghul emperors appointed 'recorders' to record their selected activities in form known as 'Namas' or chronicles. For instance, 'Nimat Nam'a and 'Shahi Nama' were written in the fifteenth century. Babur's life is recorded in 'Babur Nama'. Several Namas were prepared during

Akbar's rule, such as, '*Tuti Nama*', '*Hamza Nama*', and '*Timur Nama*'. Akbar's Laws are recorded in '*Ain-I-Akbari*'. Jahanghir's life is recorded in '*Tuzuk-I-Jahangiri*' whereas Shah Jahan's life is recorded in '*Padshah Nama*'[2].

Ibn Batuta of Arabia came to India in the tenth century CE. He has meticulously chronicled the social, political and cultural life of India. Ibn Batuta travelled to India from Morocco in 1325 CE, and wrote extensively about the Turkish rule and the Delhi Sultanate in India. He studied Indian philosophy, astronomy, literature and is credited with having brought much of India's knowledge base to the Arab world. In the eleventh century CE, Al Beruni, another Arab traveler and scholar, was commissioned by "Mahmud of Ghazni to produce his monumental commentary on Indian philosophy and culture, in his search for pure knowledge..."[9]. His book, '*Kitabh hi tahqiq ma li'l-hind*' is still regarded as one of the best sources of Indian philosophy for the Arabic world.

After the arrival of the Europeans, India has been a topic of fascination for them. The first organization to collect, translate, study, and preserve Indian texts was the Asiatick Society founded in 1784, by Sir William Jones, a judge at Calcutta High Court. Many British scholars, such as, Nathaniel Halhed, Charles Wilkins, and Governor General Warren Hastings, with Indian scholars, such as, Prasanna Thakur, Dwarkanath Tagore, Shibchandra Das, Rasamoy Datta and Ram Kumar Sen, were the founding members of this institution. In 1899, it was renamed the Asiatic Society of Bengal, and in 1950, it was changed to Asiatic Society. Asiatic Society collected and published Indian texts in Sanskrit, Arabic, Pesian, Bangali and Tibetan under *Bibliotheca Indica* series. The Society's library and archives have valuable collection of original and translated books. The work of this Society had, and continues to have, a tremendous impact on the intellectual world of India.

Many books have been written by British historians and missionaries, such as, F. W. Maitland and Lord Acton starting to write "Cambridge Modern History" and "Cambridge History of British Empire" in 1899. Some other notable British historians are Lord Macaulay, Mountstuart Elphinstone, and James Mill[8]. Many Indian historians, such as Ramesh Chandra Majumdar, Dr. Ishwari Prasad, and Lokmanya Tilak, have contributed much in this area as well.

Chapter VI
ANCIENT CIVILIZATIONS

The earliest established history of India begins in the Indus Valley around 3000-2000 BCE. All five locations of Mohen-Jo-Daro and Harappa regions, where archaeological ruins have been found, have provided enough information to establish that this civilization had well planned cities with brick houses, great baths and underground sewage systems. There is evidence that the people used copper and bronze to make weapons and ornaments. These cities "are thought to be the twin poles of civilisation which dates alongside the earliest known civilisation of Egypt and Mesopotamia. Twice the size of the Old Kingdom of Egypt, the Indus culture extended over huge area, far larger than any other ancient civilisation"[3]. Unfortunately, this civilization simply declined and vanished around 1700 BC. No definite causes of their decline have been established, but among some possible causes mentioned are climatic changes, natural disaster, and tectonic changes. This civilization had not much long-lasting effect on Indians but has remained as an item of great pride for them.

In the south, there was the Dravidian civilization, even before the advent of the Aryans. In the beginning, "... these ancient peoples of Dravidian culture included populations of the Indus and Ganges Basins as a whole, as well as those of central India"[1]. They might have been absorbed by the Aryan civilization in the north, but prospered separately in the south. However, this process of Aryan domination did not take place by force or subjugation, but by cultural exchange. "With the horse and chariot by way of dazzling new technology, and with subtleties of ritual sacrifice as a mesmerizing ideology, the 'arya' may have secured recognition of their superiority by a process no more deliberate and menacing than social attraction and cultural osmosis"[1].

The southern part of India was isolated from the north by the Deccan Plateau and Vindhya Mountain Ranges. The Dravidian civilization was later based in the region south of Narmada stretching up to the oceans.

Proximity of oceans and fertile river valley very much influenced the early development in this area. Rice and spices were abundantly produced in this area found their way through trade to the eastern Asian empires and to ancient Rome as well. "Ptolemy in second century CE mentions not only the ports of southern India but also the capitals of rulers located some distance off the coast"[3]. Unlike the northern plains, this area had developed urbanized centers and as city states. Trade and farm produce enabled this area to develop states and move from nomadic stage to statehood in a relatively short time. During the last century of BCE and first century CE, this area "...witnessed a process of urbanisation and state formation which had taken place three centuries earlier in the Gangetic region"[2].

Around 1500 BCE, there was a new civilization in India based on a tribe called 'Aryans'. It is one of the most important epochs in Indian history. The importance of the rise of Aryan civilisation and its effect on Indian history cannot be overestimated. "The Aryans brought with them new ideas, new technology, new gods, and new languages. It is the source of many essential characteristics of Indian civilisation; the roots of Indian religion, its philosophy, its literature and its customs all derive from this period"[7].

There are two distinct theories about the origin of the Aryans. Some, such as, Friederich Max Muller and Sir William Jones, noted linguistic similarities between Sanskrit, the language of the Aryans, and Greek, Latin, and German languages. They theorised that the Aryans were "a semi-nomadic people, which called itself 'Arya' in its sacred hymns came down to the northwestern plains through the mountain passes of Afghanistan"[3]. But, according to Mountstuart Elphinstone, a scholar of the East Indian Company in 1786, the Aryans were always in India, because no trace of such migration is available. He asserted that, "it was quite incredible that the Aryans could have made the transition from mountain desert to monsoonal paradise and yet fail to record it"[2]. This question of "migrating in or spreading out" of Aryans is still being debated among scholars.

Aryans had tamed horses and built chariots with two wheels with spokes. "This new type of chariot was far in advance of anything the ancient world had yet seen",[7]. More information of the Aryans comes from the Vedas and the epics *Ramayana* and *Mahabharata*. "The text of Rig Veda- a remarkable document about Aryan life, society and religion-

...These poems, together with their laws, customs, mythology, and so on, were thus transmitted by oral tradition until the time when the Aryans learned the art of writing"[1]. The epics describe not only Aryan life style, but chronicle the type of civic and social order, administrative structure, education system, customs and rituals, and ethics they followed. The epics also narrate two great wars where many kings participated, one in Kuruksetra in northern India, and the other in (Sri) Lanka in the south. At this time, Aryans had settled in the Gangetic Plain, and had the leisure of concentrating on philosophy, literature and spirituality. In short, the Vedic lifestyle was in place in this region, by this time known as 'Aryavarta' or 'the land of the Aryans'.

Aryans advanced to eastern India, and settled in the entire northern region. River Ganges played an important role in Aryan civilization. Soon this "led to the emergence of the first historical kingdoms and to a second phase of urbanization- the first being of the Indus Valley civilization[3]. By the sixth century BCE, some major states were developed. At first, tribal settlements or 'Janapada' (house of people) were developed, followed by sixteen 'Mahajanapada', or major settlements. These (delete 'that') have been mentioned in the early written texts called Puranas, or 'ancients'. Some of these settlements, such as, Rajagriha, Varanasi, Kausambi, Sravasti, Champa, Avanti, and Taxila, grew to be city states. Some of these city states still exist as cities with their original names.

Aryans did not build palaces or monuments. "Their houses, fashioned of bamboo or light wood, have not survived the ravages of time; they baked no bricks, built no elaborate baths or sewage systems, created no magnificent statues or even modest figures"[8]. They did not "conquer" nature, but lived with nature; appreciating and enjoying, being nurtured and protected.

During this period, in the process of expansion, urbanization and integration of the new group of people in one kingdom, a complex system of social order was developed, which was mistakenly called the "caste system" by the Portuguese, who were the first Europeans to come to India. In fact, it was a "class" or 'Varna' system of grouping people according to their contribution to society: *Brahmana, Ksatriya, Vaishya*, and *Shudra*[8].

Around 540 BCE, the kingdom of Magadha became the most powerful and the wealthiest of all kingdoms. "Under the kings Bimbisara (543-491 BCE) and Ajatsatru (491-461 BCE), Magadha introduced a strong administration resulting in prosperity. In fourth century BCE, it attained the peak of its glory during the reign of Mahapada Nandy of Nanda dynasty",[7]. During this time, Buddhism and Jainism prospered not only in India, but beyond its boundary to the Far East. Shortly after this period, after 320 BCE, the Maurya dynasty emerged with a large kingdom and competent rulers.

PART III
DEVELOPMENT OF INDIAN HERITAGE

Chapter VII
INVASIONS AND SETTLEMENTS

Around sixth century BCE, the Ganges Basin area of India was being urbanized, and small city kingdoms were established. These small kingdoms worked on a democratic system, and the local administration centered upon the welfare of its inhabitants. They ignored military preparedness and were blissfully unaware of the threat of foreign invasions. During this time, two important incidents took place. One was the rise of Buddhism and other invasions into India, mainly from middle Asia. From now on, an interesting phase dominated for the next fifteen hundred years. Large kingdoms and dynasties were established by great conquerors and competent rulers which were destroyed by foreign invasions, internal conflicts, inadequate military preparedness, and weak descendents. The period of large kingdoms was followed by fragmentation of such kingdoms into smaller, regional kingdoms.

King Darius of Persia was the first to invade India. He invaded the Indus Valley in 522 BCE. He did not rule this part for a long time, and when Alexander the Great of Macedonia invaded India, this part was ruled by Indian kings. The Persian invasion established a contact of Persian culture with Indian culture, and the door for Indian commerce opened to the Middle East and Rome. The Persian style of erecting pillars and slabs with royal edicts was later followed by Indian rulers. Indian rulers, particularly Chandragupta Maurya, learned the advantages of large kingdoms.

The next invasion came in 334 BCE, when Alexander's army entered Taxila, a small kingdom in the northern part of India. Ambi, the king of Taxila, welcomed him and helped him against his battle with King Porus or Purusottama, who ruled a small kingdom between the Chinab and Jhelum Rivers in an area which is presently called Punjab. This was the beginning of an odious Indian tradition, where a ruler helped an invader against his neighbor. After a valiant effort, King Purusottama was finally defeated and imprisoned. After defeating Porus, Alexander wanted to move on, but his army heard about the mighty kingdom of Magadha, and revolted. Alexander was forced to stop and return. The most important effect of Alexander's expedition was that India came in direct contact with an advanced European culture.

Around 320 BCE, Chandragupta Maurya established Maurya Dynasty, after defeating Nanda, the king of Magadha. Maurya Dynasty lasted until 185 BCE, when several groups of invaders and settlers poured in. The effects of this Dynasty are detailed in the next chapter. Around 320 BCE, this Dynasty was established in the north western part of India by Chandragupta Marya, who is regarded as "the first real emperor of India"[5].

The Maurya Dynasty ended with the fragmentation of the kingdom after invasions of Shakas, Kushans, and Pallavas. These groups came from central Asia and ruled the northern part of India for five centuries. Two rulers of these groups, Shashanka and Kanishka, accepted Buddhist religion and had significant impact into Indian history[2]. Kanishka and Shashanka had lasting effect on India's culture. Kanishka was also a great administrator, and he patronized arts and culture. Under his rule, Buddhism spread to China, Japan and Tibet. After his death, his successors were too weak and finally Chandragupta Vikramaditya came to power and established the Gupta Dynasty around 320 CE.

The period of Gupta rule is called the "Golden Age" of Indian history, because during this time philosophy and literature, science and mathematics, education and administrative systems were fostered. More about this period is covered in a later chapter. This period came to an end when Huns invaded India around 520 CE. Gupta kings were Buddhists, and practised 'Ahimsa' or nonviolence, according to the Buddhist doctrine, and shunned military preparedness. Eventually, the Huns invaded, and the Gupta dynasty came to an end. "The barbarians (Huns) of the fifth and sixth centuries constitute a turning point in the history of Northern and Western India, both political and social. They shattered Gupta empire and thus prepared the ground for the growth of a number of new states"[4].

Around 711 CE, Pravakar Bardhan, the king of Kanauj established Bardhan dynasty. King Harsha of this dynasty ruled effectively until he was defeated in 609 CE by Pulakeshin of Chalukya Dyanasty of Karnataka, a kingdom in south India. This was followed by a period of rise and fall of regional kingdoms and interregional conflicts.

From this time on, followers of many religions and sects, such as Judeic, Zoroastrian, Bahai and Ismaili, settled in India, many to take refuge from persecution from their land of origin. Not only did they live without persecution, they also became a part of the larger Indian community, contributing and enriching it in return. Members of these communities participated and provided leadership in the struggle for India's independence, and reached very high position in government, military and industry. Some of them assimilated few "Hindu" practices through cultural diffusion, but all of them have kept their original faith strong.

Judaism was the first 'non-Dharmic' religion to arrive India. The first group of Jewish people came to India around 2500 years ago and settled in the coast of Cochin. Therefore, they were called 'The Cochin Jews'. The largest community of Jewish settlers in India is called Bene Israel. They are regarded as descendents of the Ten Lost Tribes. Around fourth century CE, Jewish traders contributed much to the ancient kingdom of Kudungallur near Kerala in India. As a token of gratitude, King Parkaran Vanmar, the ruler of this kingdom, gave to the head of the Jewish community, Joseph Rabban, the village of Anjuvannam and pronounced him the Prince of this village. These Jewish rulers had all the rights preserved for the ruling families of the Indian kingdoms. Some Jewish settlers lived along the Malabar coast, where they traded peacefully until 1524, when the Muslim invaders destroyed their settlements. At present, there are over three dozen thriving Synagogues in India. About half of all Jews live in Manipur, and about a quarter live in Mumbai. According to Jewish historians, the Jewish settlers lived in India free of any anti-Semitism from the Hindus, but did face attacks first from Muslim invaders, and later from the Portuguese, who wanted to convert them to Christianity.

The Zoroastrians, fleeing from Islamic persecution in Persia, landed in the Sanjan area of India, sometimes between 936 CE or 716 CE, but the exact date is still disputed. Jadav Rana, the ruler of Sanjan, let them settle, and for their land of origin Persia, they were called the Parsis. They built their first temple in 721 CE, and lived peacefully without persecution. In time, they settled in other parts of India, prospering and contributing as farmers, weavers, and carpenters. In 1465, Muslim invaders destroyed their temples in Sanjan, and after a valiant fight, they took refuge in caves with sacred fire. In Thana, Portuguese rulers considered them to be idolaters, and they were put upon by missionaries to convert to Christianity. The Parsis in India are well known for being highly educated and leaders of industry and the military.

The Ismailis are part of Muslim Shiites and a subsection of the Nizar sect, which originated in the eleventh century, after the death of the sixth Shiite Imam. They moved to India in 1840 under the leadership of Aga Khan. In Syria and Iran, the Nizars were considered to be assassins in crusades. Most Ismaiilis settled in the Sindh and Gujarat areas of India.

Bahai faith was founded in 1844 by a young man in Siraz, Persia, called Baab. India has been associated with the Bahai faith since its inception. During the first year, Baab appointed one of his followers as the leader of Bahais in India. Bahais live in India in over ten thousand localities, and are a strong force in working for peace and harmony.

The political fragmentation and lure of riches in India became a fertile ground for further invasions. Around 1000 CE, Mahmud of Ghazni in central Asia, an Islamic invader, began raiding India. Until 1026, Mahmud invaded India seventeen times, and each time his army looted temples, palaces and monasteries. In 1192, another invader, Mahmud of Ghaur defeated the Rajput king, Prithwiraj Chauhan, and established Turkish Sultan rule in India. After three centuries of Turkish rule, the Mughul Empire was established in 1526 when Babur defeated Ibrahim Lodhi, the last Sultan of Delhi. The Mughuls ruled India for three centuries, until British rule began in 1757. The British, similar to other European groups, came to India to trade, but gradually became rulers of India. Unlike other groups, Islamic invaders and the British settled in India for a prolonged period of occupation and colonization, but never assimilated into the mainstream of India.

Historians fail to comprehend the reasons how a culturally advanced society could be invaded, conquered and colonized by so many foreign powers. History shows that whenever there was disunity among Indians and India was politically fragmented, India was invaded and consequently defeated. Indian soldiers were neither disciplined nor properly trained to face war-hardened soldiers of invading armies, inspired by religious fervor and motivated by the possibility of acquiring riches by plundering and looting. Indians rode elephants against soldiers on horses, which were more mobile, particularly in a rain- drenched battle field. Fighting was left for a small group of people belonging to the 'Ksatriys' or caste of Indian society, leaving the rest of the population unprepared for battles. Also, Indians had no standing armies. Many Indian rulers were Buddhists, and followed the principle of 'Ahimsa' or non-violence. All these factors caused Indians to be defeated so many times. The effects of these historical developments are still felt in India.

The most remarkable aspect of these developments is the fact that Indian culture not only survived but always prospered during invasions and occupations, and their social and cultural institutions remained intact. The culture of India was only enriched and reformed by the assimilation of so many alien cultures. However, the economic sector suffered greatly during the oppression of Islamic rule and exploitation during the British rule[1.]

Each of these invasions affected political, social and cultural aspects of India. As stated before, Indian rulers established large kingdoms after the Persian and Greek invasions, and reorganized their administrative systems. From the Greeks, Indian rulers learned the art of erecting pillars and stone edicts, inscribing royal proclamations. Through the Kushans, India came in contact with Rome, and the trade started. This was the beginning of the 'Silk Route'. During the rule of Kanishka, great progress was made in the field of culture. Philosophers such as Nagarjuna, Ashwaghosh, and Basumitra developed their treaties in Sanskrit. Patanjali developed another form of Samskrit grammar. Charaka and Susruta enriched the 'Ayurvedic' system of medical treatment. Temples with magnificent sculptures and beautiful architectures were erected in Sarnath, Amaravati and Mathura.

Most historians belive that some of the invading warrior groups who settled in India formed and helped the rise of the Rajputs or 'princes' group in India. Many Rajput rulers were skilled warriors and they fought valiantly with Muslim occupiers, and became known for their bravery. This aspect is covered in upcoming chapters.

These invasions, migrations and settlements have also resulted in the formation of several distinct anthropological groupings in India. In 1890, Herbert Hope Rieley, an official in British India, classified races in India on the basis of their facial features and physical build. According to him, there were there five distinct racial groups: Indo-Aryans, Scytho-Dravidians with Sakas and Dravidians, Aryo-Dravidians with Aryans and Dravidians, Mongolo-Dravidians with Mongoloids and Dravidians, Mongoloids and Dravidians. Later, other anthropologists, such as, Giuffrid and Ruggeri (1921), Hadden (1924), Eickstead (1934), and Guha (1931), have disputed these classifications, and each of them have presented their own version of racial classification of Indians[3].

Chapter VIII
EARLY KINGDOMS AND DYNASTIES

The first large kingdom emerged in India in 324 BCE, when Chandragupta defeated Dhanananda, the last of Nanda kings of Magadha, with the help of a Brahmin scholar, Kautilya.   Chandragupta continued to conquer other smaller kingdoms of north India and came face to face with Seleukus, the governor of the Greek-occupied part of the Indus Valley. He married the daughter of Seleukus and established the Maurya Kingdom, and took the name of Chandragupta Maurya. A detailed account of his reign is chronicled by Megasthenes, a Greek official in his court and by Kautilya in his book, '*Arthashstra*'. "Maurya empire was probably the most extensive ever forged by an Indian Dynasty",[1].

Chandragupta's empire extended from Bengal to Afghanistan and from the Himalayas to the Vindhya Mountain Ranges. He was a competent ruler, and initiated a well designed administrative system, with governors, superintendents, treasury officers, and executive officers. His judicial system was fair. He gave special attention to the welfare of the public, and was greatly admired by them. His ministers were wise, competent and loyal.

Chandragupta's son, Bindusara became king after him, and continued to rule with the same competence. In 273 BCE, his son, Ashoka, became the emperor, and is regarded as one of the best rulers of India. Ashoka lived according to the principles of Buddhism. In addition to maintaining an efficient administrative system, great progress in the realm of culture was made during his reign. He is most known for his service to Buddhist religion. He erected edicts, pillars and inscriptions, which included messages of service to all, respect for the elders, religious toleration, non-violence, truthfulness, and charity. These inscriptions describe much of his personality and character. He gave up the luxuries of being a king, and lived the life of a monk. He introduced measures to improve the lives of his subjects. During his rule, Indian literature, arts and architecture made great progress.

The effect of the Maurya dynasty on Indian culture was deep and widespread. During this period, architecture, sculpture, engineering, and jewelry made great progress. Royal palaces, shrines of Buddhism or 'Stupas', monasteries were constructed throughout India. Asoka's pillars constituted of huge sculptures of fine statues carved out of huge single rock. The most famous one is a pillar with four lions, which has been adopted by India as the national emblem. Much attention was paid to education, and numerous schools or 'Gurkuls' were established for public education. A university at Taxila is regarded as one of the oldest universities in the world, which continued to exist for several centuries as the prime center of higher education. Literary works also prospered during this period. Kautilya's *'Arthasastra'* and Bhadra Banus *'Kalpasutra'* are some examples of great works of literature. "Bindusara's son Asoka, one of the most famous figures in Indian history and one of the great names of all ages, ruled unchallenged for thirty-seven years over the greatest empires had ever seen,"[3].

After Ashoka, his successors were too weak, the kingdom became too large to be efficiently administered, and eventually the Brahmins revolted against the state patronage of Buddhism. According to the teachings of Buddhism, *'Ahimsa'* or non-violence was practiced, and military preparedness was ignored. Finally, the invasion by the Shakas, and uprising by the Sunga rulers, the great Maurya Dynasty came to an end. For the next five centuries, India was fragmented into smaller kingdoms which fought with each other. However, culture continued to flourish in spite of political turmoil and instability. "Thus the much maligned 'dark period' was actually the harbinger of the classical age",[2].

In 320 CE, Chandragupta I inherited a small polity near Magadha. He acquired more territories by conquests and by marriage. His son, Samudragupta, extended the kingdom and established the Gupta Dynasty. His kingdom extended the entire region of 'Aryavarta',[2]. In 409 CE, his son Chandragupta II conquered the Sakas, and extended the kingdom to the south. Chandragupta II took the title of 'Vikramaditya', and in regarded as one of the most efficient warriors and rulers of India. His son, Kumargupta, faced the invasion by the Huns, and war with Pushyamitra. These two events weakened the kingdom. Skandagupta, Kumargupta's son, continued to fight the Huns, and was able to save his Kingdom. After Skandagupta's death, history repeated itself, and the great Gupta Dynasty came to an end due to the same reasons as the fall of the Maurya Dynasty

Fa Hien, the Buddhist pilgrim from China, wrote a detailed account of Gupta rule. According to him, "The people are well off, without tax or official restrictions". His description of Magadha is more impressive, "Its towns were the largest and its people the richest and most prosperous as well the most virtuous".

The Gupta Dynasty introduced a political unity in India with a feeling of nationalism. His kingdom erased all regional powers, and freed all areas from invaders. Material prosperity was spread while maintaining a moral life. Guptas established an ideal type of government. Hinduism was revived, and Sanskrit was studied again. Religious harmony was maintained as many high officials in the court were Buddhists and Jainists.

For this revival, and its importance for India's culture, this period is also known as "The Classical Age"[2].

Chandragupta Vikramaditya had a group of nine talented and learned men in his court, known as 'Navaratna' or nine gems, who contributed much in many areas of culture. Kalidasa, a poet and dramatist, wrote several books, Varahamira, the astronomer, calculated the movements of celestial bodies. Aryabhatta, the mathematician, wrote several treaties on mathematics which made great strides in the area of science and mathematics. Music, Art and Sculpture were also encouraged. The iron pillar, erected in this period, contains practically no carbon, and is still free of any rust even after being exposed to rain and sun for over a thousand years. Some works of art have survived, but many were deliberately destroyed by Moghul rulers, mainly by the Emperor Aurangzeb. During Gupta rule, trade and commerce flourished, and exports went to the Far East and to Rome as well. This period witnessed such a greatness and glory, that it is an issue of great pride and a source of nationalism for many Indians. "The rule of the Guptas saw a new empire which was to dominate the whole of northern India. It lasted for almost 150 years and saw such as brilliance outpouring of science, art, music, and literature that it has been hailed as the 'Golden Age' of classical India",[3].

Keeping up the historical tradition, the mighty the Gupta Dynasty fell for the same reasons that the Maurya dynasty collapsed, and the kingdom fragmented again into smaller kingdoms. However, another powerful and effective dynasty, the Vardhan Dynasty, emerged when Harsha became a ruler of Thaneswar, a small kingdom in northern India. Soon, he spread his rule to Malwa, and continued to expand his kingdom. He defeated Sashanka, the ruler of Bengal, and conquered many smaller kingdoms in the north, and then even continued to conquer kingdoms in the south.

Most information about Harsha and his rule is found in '*Harsha Charita*', written by Banbhatta. Chinese monk Fa Hien has also described his rule. Both of these sources reveal that Harsha was not only a great conqueror he was also an effective and competent ruler. He is considered to be a Hindu in the beginning, but embraced Buddhism in his later life. He assembled Buddhist scholars, and organized assemblies for religious and philosophical discourses. He patronized scholars in his court, such as Bana, Matanga, Jaysena and Bhatri Hari. These scholars, who contributed much to the Indian culture, are still admired. Harsha continued to maintain the great universities of Nalanda and Taxila. Nalanda University, according to Fa Hien, had three storied buildings, over one hundred classrooms for ten thousand students from all over India, the Far East and Tibet. It also had three libraries and several buildings as student residences. Harsha is regarded as a worthy successor of the Mauryas and the Guptas. "The size and splendor of his empire make it appear as if Harsha were a latter day replica of the great Gupta rulers",[2].

Shortly after Harsha's death, his dynasty came to an end, the ancient Indian empires disappeared, and for the next one thousand years India remained fragmented. However, during this period, many regional kingdoms emerged with competent and effective rulers, as described in the next chapter.

Chapter IX
SMALL KINGDOMS

As stated before, no ruler has ever ruled over entire India, and over half of India has been ruled by a single ruler only six times, and only for less than four hundred years out of five thousand years of history. There were many smaller kingdoms in existence not only when large kingdoms broke down, but also during their rule. This was more prominent in south India, as this region was mostly isolated by the Bindhyachal Mountain Ranges from the north. These kingdoms were ruled by some very effective rulers who managed to strengthen culture and instill religious harmony. Almost all of them patronized literature and the arts, and built temples and erected sculptures. During this time, great buildings were built, art and literature prospered, philosophy and ethics developed, science and mathematics advanced. "In the centuries followed by the Gupta period it was in the kingdoms of the Chalukyas, Rastrakutas, Pallavs and Cholas that Indian civilization showed its greatest vitality",[1]. Unfortunately, since these rulers were following Buddhist and Hindu teachings, they neglected military preparedness, and were unable to withstand foreign invasions.

North India had many kingdoms in the area ranging from Banga (Bengal) in the east to the Indus Valley in the west. According to Buddhist and Jain texts, several small kingdoms existed during 650 to 325 BCE, such as, the Sakyas of Kapilvastu, Mallas of Kushinagar, and Lichchavis of Vaisali. Most of these kingdoms were ultimately conquered by the Mauryas of Magadha. During this time, Buddhist texts were created and preserved, and much of Pali literature was developed. These kingdoms also worked on democratic lines, and were less ready to react to invasions.

After the disintegration of the Maurya Empire, Pusyamitra Sunga, a commander of the Maurya army established the Sunga dynasty. It lasted from 187 to 75 BCE. The importance of this period is that Bramhanism or Hinduism regained prominence again, and Sanskrit was revived. Under the patronage of the king, the famous book on Hindu customs and law,

'*Manusmriti*', and a book on Sanskrit grammar by Patanjali were written. "The Sunga period, lasting one hundred and twelve years, was as is often in case in times of political disorganization marked by a great flourishing of the arts. The kings encouraged literature and the sciences",[2].

The Andhara kings ruled from 28 BCE to 225 CE, and there were several competent rulers who patronized the creation of Puranas, and the Prakrit language prospered during their rule. Foreign trade also expanded, and temples and other religious institutions of both Hindu and Buddhist religions were constructed.

The Sakas were originally employed by the Parthian rulers as '*Satraps*' or viceroys. The first Saka ruler was a Satrap of Taxila in first century BCE, and later other small kingdoms of Sakas were established in Nasik, Mathura and Ujjain. Sakas ruled for over four centuries, and the most famous ruler was Rudradaman. He ruled from 120 to 150 CE, and his kingdom spread over most of north India. Rudradaman was a great patron of art and literature. He behaved like a constitutional monarch instead of an absolute one. Eventually, Sakas were absorbed in Indian society and later became great a source of Indian resistance against foreign rule. "Sakas remained a warrior people and later played an important role in the struggle against the Muslim and then British invaders',[2].

The next significant rulers were the Kushans. Originally from China, Kushans, or 'Kouei-Chouang', defeated other tribes of northwestern India around 40 CE, and established Kushan rule. Among all the Kushan rulers, Kanishka is the most striking figure. He ascended the throne in 120 CE, and ruled for forty years. He was a great warrior, and conquered up to Kasmir in the north, Magadha in the east, Punjab and Mathura in the west. He also annexed three provinces of China. He was an able administrator, and a great patron of Buddhist religion. During his rule, Buddhist religion was reformed and spread all over India and beyond in East Asia. A large number of philosophers and scholars such as Nagarjuna and Vasumitra, and an ayurvedic physician named Charaka, were in his court. Under his tutelage, the '*Gandhar*' school of art prospered. He also built lofty towers, buildings and stupas to preserve the relics of Buddha. He even founded three cities, which still exist today. "Kanishka's fame is not only based on military and political successes but also as his spiritual merit",[3].

After Harsha's death in 647 CE, his kingdom broke into smaller kingdoms again, and from this time to the invasion and occupation by the Muslims in the twelfth century, the national unity was completely lost, and this period was dominated by the Rajputs in the north. The origin of Rajputs is still being debated. Colonel Todd, a well known historian, claims that Rajputs were originally descendents of a foreign tribe. Others historians hold that the Rajputs are Aryans. Some Rajputs believe that they are *'Suryavansi'* or descendents of the Sun god. Most historians think that Rajputs are a mixed race[4].

Rajputs ruled over smaller kingdoms in the northern part of India, such as, Delhi, Ajmer, Kanauj, Malwa, Bundelkhand, Mewar, Chedi, and Bengal. Rajputs were great warriors, but they ruled under a feudal system, and lacked political skills. They shunned political practices of conspiracies, opportunistic alliances, underhanded deals, treachery and deceit. They were honest and were ready to help out their subjects. They were proud of their families, and dealt fairly with friends and foes alike, and respected all women. Although they were Hindus, they honored all three religions, such as, Hinduism, Buddhism, and Jainism. However, during this time, Sankaracharya, a prominent religious reformer, revived Bramhanism, which spread all over India, replacing Buddhism and Jainism. Rajputs built beautiful palaces and temples, which are still objects of tourist attraction. "The Rajput period was the most extraordinary era of Hindu architecture and sculpture",[2]. However, Rajputs were not united among themselves, had no feelings of nationalism, and they lacked a national hero who could unite them. As a result they could not survive the Muslim onslaught, in spite of their bravery and skill as great warriors. Even in defeat, they showed great bravery and strength of character. "They stood, at any event, as the vanguard of Hindu Indians spirited opposition to the Muslim conquest, and even when defeated in battle or driven from one desert fortress to another, they never completely surrendered",[5].

While all this was going on in the north, there were some prominent kingdoms in the south. The first one was Pallava King Vishnugupta, who was defeated by Samudragupta in 346 CE, but managed to defeat other southern rulers of Cheras, Cholas and Pandyas. For about two hundred years, from 550 to 750 CE, the Pallavas ruled over the area presently known as Madras, Trichurapalli and Tanjore. They built beautiful sculptures and pillars carved out of solid rocks. They also built temples in the style of *'Rathas'* or chariots which still exist today. "In the domain of the arts the Pallavs created an architectural style that was known as 'Dravidian'. One aspect of this style is represented by the 'mandapans'-vast roof halls supported by rows of sculptured pillars. Great bas-reliefs, sculptured in rocks or incorporated in the temples, still show the beauty of Pallava art",[2].

Chalukyas, another dynasty in the south, were the rulers of Badami from 543 to 753 CE, but were defeated by the Rastrakuts. Chalukyas came to rule from Kalyani for the second time from 973 to 1190 CE. Several rulers of this dynasty contributed much to literature and arts by their patronage, such as, the famous fresco paintings in the caves at Ajanta and Elora. They constructed many temples that exist still today. "The sculptures that decorate Chalukya temples show a unique elegance, refinement of manufacture and expansion, and are furthermore totally exempt from foreign influence",[2].

Cholas were other effective rulers in the south, presently known as Tamils. "The three Tamil kingdoms of the south seem initially to have alternated between political alliances designed to ward off their northern neighbors, and warfare among themselves",[5]. They have been mentioned in the epic *Mahabharata*, and are regarded as the most famous rulers in Tamil history. They came to prominence in the ninth century, and they defeated the Pallavs and Pandya rulers to spread their kingdom in the south. Chola administration was well organized and effective. They ruled with the help of popular assemblies, and relied on local self governments. They are best known for the temples built in Tanjore. The temples of Tanjore survived the destructive actions of the Muslim rulers, as they were too far away from Delhi, the seat of Muslim rulers. Similar to most other rulers, Cholas also patronized arts, literature and sculpture. "The Cholas were great patrons of literature and the arts. Chola era saw a considerable development of Tamil literature",[2].

Another feature of these southern rulers was that they spread Indian culture and trade to East Asia and Rome. There were even some Hindu colonies established in Java, Sumatra, Bali, Cambodia, Burma and Ceylon. Even today, much evidence of Indian religions, arts, literature and architecture are oresent in this part of this world.

PART IV

INDIAN HERITAGE THROUGH OCCUPATION

Chapter X
TURKISH INCURSIONS

In the seventh century, when Harsha was ruling peacefully and Indian culture was thriving under his patronage, Islam religion was born in Arabia. Islam preached monotheism, equality and brotherhood among all men, and absolute and unquestionable authority to 'Allah'. All teachings of Islam are recorded in the Koran. "The monotheistic conception lends this feeling of superiority a kind of divine sanction...This is what leads monotheistic peoples to be aggressive, intolerant, and destructive",[2]. Further, "The equivocal monotheism of Islam served to unite all Muslims into a brotherhood that was at once a mighty social as well as a military force",[5]. Islam is now a world religion with over a billion followers. Introduction of Islam changed the history of the world, and had a profound effect on India. "Not since the Aryan dispersion more than two thousand years earlier had any series of invaders had so profound an impact on South Asia as would those that brought the religion of Prophet Mohammed to Indian soil",[5]. The era of benevolent rulers was over, and soon the difficult period of invasion, occupation and oppression began. "From the moment when Muslims reached India, its history has no further interest. It is a long monotonous recital of murders, massacres, plunder, and destruction",[2].

Within a few years of the founding of Islam, tough Arab horsemen spread out to Europe, Central Asia, and then to India to conquer and amass wealth. "Armed with their faith and their spears, sure of having the only God on their side, the Arabs launched on their world conquest with enthusiasm and passion",[2]. As early as in 712 AD, Muhammad bin Kashim of Arabia invaded Sindh, or Indus region of India, but his conquest and occupation was short lived and had little effect on India, except it was known to the Arabs that India could be invaded through the Khyber Pass and easily defeated.

Scholars have wondered about the developments in India during this period. How could a small group of horsemen invade and conquer a land of culturally advanced people who were not able to defend their own land? How could these 'foreigners' rule with an iron fist and oppress a vast population for over five centuries without successful resistance and rebellion? And lastly, how could the culture of India not only survived, but thrived and prospered in spite of systematic destruction and planned oppression?

After the death of Harsha, when the Arabs invaded, India was fragmented into many smaller states. North India was mainly ruled by Rajputs, who were brave warriors, but were not united among themselves. "Dissention among the minor states and the lack of a common ideal made India an easy prey for the invaders, despite the admirable courage of most of the Indian princesses",[2]. Due to a rigid caste system, only the 'Khastrias' were supposed to defend the land. Indians' war strategy was cumbersome and based upon the use of elephants, whereas, the invaders could move swiftly on horses. The invaders had religious fanaticism on their side, and were united for a great cause. The three main Indian religions, Hinduism, Buddhism and Jainism were further fragmenting society. All these three religions shunned violence, and neglected military readiness. Most resources and effort were put for cultural enrichment. As a result only the cultural aspect was strong and advanced, depriving all other areas, particularly a strong defence against battle ready, zealous, and ruthless invaders. Perhaps, defeated and oppressed in all areas, Indians took refuge in their culture and took solace in advancing it.

Between 1001 and 1026 CE, Muhamud, the Turkish ruler of Ghazni, invaded India seventeen times, and continued plundering wealth, destroying and looting temples, slaughtering Hindus. "After each of his seventeen expeditions within South Asia, he would return to Ghazni before the summer rains, laden with booty including slaves, gold, elephants and jewels", [1]. His successors, "continued his policy of raids, destruction, and pillage...the holy city of Varanasi was sacked, and its wonderful temples systematically destroyed",[2]. His court chronicler, Uthi, wrote that in Somnath alone, "more than fifty thousand Hindus were slain that day and over two million dinars worth of gold and jewels were taken",[5]. Muhammad Ghazni not only conquered and looted palaces and temples he also destroyed them and systematically slaughtered common people. He amassed such wealth each time that his appetite to revisit strengthened. There was another side of Mahmmad Ghazni. He was a lover of Muslim culture. Several scholars, such as Al Beruni, Firdausi and Utabi, created wonderful masterpieces of literature during this period.

It was Muhammad Ghori, the ruler of Ghor, who invaded India several times during the period of 1175 to 1206. He conquered and occupied smaller kingdoms of north India and founded Muslim rule. He conquered Sind, and then moved towards central India in 1191 CE, and faced Prithviraj Chauhan, the Rajput ruler of Thaneswar. Prithviraj Chauhan, fought Muhammad Ghori and defeated him. However, Muhammad Ghori invaded again. When Prithviraj Chauhan asked other Rajput rulers to unite against Muhammad Ghori, Jai Chand, the ruler of Kanauj stayed away. Rajputs fought valiantly, and "They stood, at any event, as the vanguard of Hindu India's spirited opposition to the Muslim conquest",[5]. But, Prithiwiraj and most other Rajputs were defeated in the end. Later on Muhammad Ghori's successors defeated Jai Chand, and the main resistance in North India was over. Bengal region, which had prospered under Pala and Senas dynasties, was conquered in 1202. During this conquest of Bengal, "Nalanda University was sacked ...driving thousand of Buddhists to flee toward Nepal and Tibet and killing uncounted others who weren't swift enough to escape",[5].

In the south, there were smaller kingdoms of Rastakuts, Cholas, Chalukyas, Pandyas and Cheras. Muhammad Ghori easily defeated Gujarat in the south, but he was defeated and assissinated by Khokars, a tribe in revolt. As he had no son, his viceroy became the Sultan or 'Ruler' of Delhi, the political capital of north India. This was the beginning of the 'Slave Dynasty'. For the next four centuries, there were several Sultans of Delhi from four main dynasties: Khilji, Tughlak, Syyed, and Lodhi. These rulers continued the "strategy of plundering kingdoms and their major objective was to acquire booty",[1].

Until now, most succession of rulers has been peaceful and methodical, but the Muslim rulers practised their ruthlessness also among themselves, and most successions were results of murder and assassination, imprisonment and palace intrigue, full of conspiracies and treacheries, committed by their own family members, generals, or chieftains.

"The Muslim rule was theocratic, of which the Sultan was the temporal and religious head...The Hindu nobles were hostile and were largely massacred...Koranic law was the only law recognized",[2]. Almost all of them facilitated construction of tombs and palaces, and patronized writers to chronicle their 'glorious' rule. "The Sultan's sources of income included '*kharaj*' or taxes collected from Hindu landowners, ...and '*jijya*' or a special tax on all non-Muslims",[2].

"The Delhi sultanate reached its peak during the reign of Alauddin Khilji, around 1296-1316...He was the strongest of all Delhi sultans, centralizing power and ruthlessly suppressing all threats to his authority",[1]. Similar to previous Turkish rulers, he amassed much wealth from conquered kings. According to Amir Khusroo, his biographer, he continued "the strategy of plundering kingdoms", and his "major objective was to acquire booty". For example, to Alauddin, "20 000 horses and 100 elephants were given up by the Kakatiya king, along with the famous diamond later known as 'Koh-i-noor'. This diamond was later taken away by the British, and now is in display at the Tower of London. He introduced a wage and price control system, and checked grain prices. He divided his kingdom into small districts, or *'Sarkars'* and *'Parganas'* for better administration. Local administration was carried out by *'Sarkars'*, and this title is still in use as a last name in India. The term Sarkar in Hindi is also used for government by common folks. For tax collection, he zoned land areas into *'jagirs'*, and officials called *'jagirdars'* were appointed to collect taxes. This system was continued with different names by the Mughols and the British, the next two rulers of India. Alauddin raided Rajput kingdoms, and conquered most of them. Defeated Rajputs carried out *'jauhar'* or sacrificing themselves by walking into fire rather than surrendering to the Muslims. These episodes are still reverberated in folk songs, ballads, and legends in India.

Hindu religion and Islam were very different. "It is difficult to imagine two religious ways of life more different than Islam and Hinduism",[1]. Also, the Muslim rulers tried to destroy existing religion and culture by force. "Although these new rulers of India did identify with the country they have conquered, their faith nevertheless remained distinctly alien and this lead to conflict and tension hitherto unknown",[4]. Unlike previous invaders, Muslims mostly remained separated from the mainstream Indian society. "All previous invaders of India contributed to its culture, religion, arts, and skills. This was not the case with Muslims, whose contribution was essentially negative",[2].

Even then, some reformers tried to seek cooperation between Hindus and Muslims. Kabir (1440-1518), a Muslim by birth but a disciple of a Hindu saint Ramananda, inspired many with his mystic writing of 'love of God'. *'Sufism'*, a sect of Islam, found common ground with *'Bhaktism'* a sect based on devotion to God in Hinduism, as both of them stressed 'love for God'. In Bengal, the Bhakti movement was advanced by the teachings of Chaitanya (1485-1533).

In Punjab, Nanak (1469-1518), became the first 'Guru' or teacher, who preached a doctrine of ongoing devotion to the 'One God, the Creator' whose name is Truth or '*Sat*', to his '*Sikhs*' or disciples. This was the fourth world religion developed in India, "This religion became a martial one, with subsequent Gurus driven to take up sword by Mughal persecution",[5].

Eventually, the Turkish Sultanate was weakened by inept successors and the invasion of Tamerlane, a Mongol warrior, in 1398. He wanted to conquer the world, spread Islam all over the world, and loot the wealth of India. He conquered Delhi and let loose mass killings and plundering by his soldiers. However, he did not stay in India and left with huge loot. In 1526, when Ibrahim Lodhi was the ruler of Delhi, his governor of Lahore got upset with him, and invited Babur, the ruler of Kabul to invade India. Babur defeated Ibrahim Lodhi, the last Turkish Sultan of India, and the Mughal dynasty began in India which lasted for almost three centuries.

Chapter XI
MOGHUL OCCUPATION

The term 'Moghul dynasty' conjures up a period of splendor and romance, immortalized in 'Taj Mahal', a mausoleum created by emperor Shah Jahan for his wife Mumtaj, a work of art and love. However, the Moguls have a curious legacy. They established a dynasty after defeating Lodhi rulers in Delhi and later conquering smaller kingdoms in Northern India. Most Moghul rulers continued the practice of plundering and destroying palaces, cities and temples. Many of them occupied thrones by imprisoning and assassinating their own family members. They lived in luxury, and in spite of this violent character, also patronized art, music and literature, and built magnificent palaces, gardens and mausoleums. Historians have wondered about this contradiction:

"The great Mughals, whose reigns in the entire seventeenth century, have, with good reason, became a universal symbol of power and affluence, tenderness and cruelty, of ferocity and sensitivity: luxury loving, licentious, sentimental, brutal, and poetic, they were the embodiment of all those extremes characteristic of the Indian life-style known as Mughlai",[4].

The founder of Moghul dynasty was Babur, a warlord on the border of Persia and Uzbekistan. Babur, or 'Lion' in Turkish, was descendant of both Timerlane and Ghengis Khan. Therefore he possessed the Persian art of the use of firearms and quick cavalry warfare of the Uzbeks. These two skills served him well, when he invaded India in 1526 and defeated Ibrahim Lodhi in a decisive battle at Panipat near Delhi. "Babur's mobile artillery was a striking innovation for India....light-weight artillery and muskets were new to India, and they gave Babur a decisive advantage over his adversaries",[3]. This easily mobile artillery and his skillful military tactics brought him victories against the Turkish Sultans, and later against the Rajputs, who ruled several smaller kingdoms in north India. Within a few years of his invasion, Babur founded a dynasty, which produced many effective, competent but ruthless rulers.

Although from different geographical and ethnic origins, Moghul rulers continued to follow the similar style of rule as of the Turkish rulers they defeated. Their rule was mainly resisted by the Rajputs and Afghans in the north, and Bahmani and Marathas in the south. Most fierce resistance came from Rana Sanga, the Rajput prince of Mewar. Rana had survived years of Turkish rule, and was a proud warrior. In the first battle against Babur, he was victorious, but finally he was defeated. Babur proved to be an effective warrior. He was also a lover of literature and was a poet himself. He built tombs and mosques, often destroying Hindu temples, including the now infamous Babri mosque. He is most known for building several beautiful gardens with fountains and channels of flowing water. His biography, 'Babur Nama', reveals most information about him. However, Babur was not an able kingdom builder, and after his death, his fragile administration was left to his weak son, Humayun.

Although Humayun conquered a few smaller kingdoms, he proved to be a weak ruler. He was ousted and exiled by one of his Afghan generals, Sher Khan. Sher Khan crowned himself as 'Sher Shah' or emperor, and turned out to be competent ruler. He amassed extraordinary wealth through looting and marriage alliances, and introduced an effective administrative system. He divided his kingdom into 'Subas' or provinces, appointing 'Subadars' or governors to rule over them. He further divided the provinces into 'Jagirs' or districts, and appointed 'Jagirdars' to collect taxes. This way, revenue collection was secured, and only these middlemen faced the wrath of the taxpayers. This system proved to be convenient for the rulers, and was adopted by the Moghuls, and later perfected by the British in their system of 'indirect rule', described in later chapters. Sher Shah "revitalised every aspect of administration by taking personal interest in all appointments to positions of power, consolidating central authority over outlining districts, and designing a blueprint for more efficient imperial rule",[3]. He is famous for constructing a long road with 'sarais' or inns from one end to the other of his kingdom, now known as the Grand Trunk Road. He also introduced an efficient postal system in India. Sher Shah ruled only for five years, dying soon in an accident during a battle. His successors proved to be weak rulers, and soon Humayun regained the kingdom. Humayun died soon after, and the kingdom was passed over to his son, Akbar.

Akbar proved to be one of the best rulers in Indian history. "Many consider Akbar the most brilliant emperor of the Mughal house, while others include him among South Asia's three greatest leaders"[1]. Most opposition to his rule came from the Rajputs, particularly from Rana Pratap of Chitor. Akbar eventually conquered most of India, but unlike other conquerors, he treated the defeated rulers with respect. Akbar even appointed Hindus as administrators, and Hindu scholars were invited to his court. This gesture, particularly towards the Rajputs, won him much cooperation and respect in return. "Akbar sought to make the Rajputs active participants in the enterprise of empire. These Hindu warriors became segment of the Indian-born nobility that Akbar recruited...",[1]. Akbar's genius was that he included both Hindus and Muslims into his inner circle of power. Hindu poets, such as Todermal and Birbal were invited to his court, and they helped Akbar rule more effectively. Akbar reversed the trend of oppression of Hindus, and stopped the *'jijiya'* tax imposed only on non-Muslims. He invited leaders of all religions into his court and tried to introduce a universal religion *'Din I Ilahi'*. He patronized art and music, and built many magnificent palaces. Akbar's effort to fuse both the Persian and Indian cultures produced a unique form of Moghul arts, which is still admired and fostered in India. Urdu, a language so called because it was first used by the soldiers in uniform or 'Urdi', built on the fusion of Sanskrit and Persian, was developed during this time. Urdu later prospered into a language with a rich literature, although Persian remained the court language during Moghul rule.

Akbar introduced a sound administrative system, dividing the provinces into *'Mansabs'* or districts. These were ruled by *'Mansandars'* replacing the *'Jagirdars'*. The army was led by *'Fauzdars'* and *'Habildars'*. *'Dar'* in Persian means 'Chief' or 'Head'. These titles are still in use in India, with their English and Sanskrit/Hindi equivalent terms. He also introduced the *'Zamindar'* or landlord system, where both Hindu and Muslim middlemen collected revenues from the peasants. These zamindars could maintain their own forces, and had to live off their lands. As a result, the farmers often suffered, particularly when the harvest was meager, but the coffer of the kingdom enhanced, and the zamindars lived in luxury, oppressing the farmers. This system was maintained by the British. Even today, many government officials in India consider it to be their right to demand additional revenues for themselves, from the public whom they are supposed to serve. In reality, it is a form of extortion and a bribe, and thus a crime under the Indian penal code. In spite of being a crime, it is still practised by many officials and euphemistically called a *'pagri', 'selami', 'baksis', 'bhet', 'ghus',* or *'upri',* depending on the local language or slang.

Akbar's son, Jehangir became the Emperor after poisoning Akbar. He continued to spread Moghul kingdom by conquering more areas. His wife, Nur Jahan had a great influence on him, and is regarded by many historians to be the 'real ruler' of that time. He was also a patron of art and literature. During his rule, European merchants initiated trade with India for cloth, indigo, spices, and timber. Jahangir granted a *'farman'* or royal permission to the British merchants to trade in India. His son, Shahjahan, became ruler after he killed all his rivals to the throne, and chased Nur Jahan away from Delhi.

Shah Jahan's rule is regarded as the 'Golden period' of Moghul rule. His kingdom was the largest in the world at that time, and he immersed himself in luxury and glory. He is famous for 'Taj Mahal', a mausoleum he built for his departed wife, Mumtaj. He also built the peacock throne, which was looted and taken away to Persia by the Persian invader Nadir Shah, and is still in Iran. Shah Jahan was imprisoned by his third son Aurangzeb, who also killed his brothers to become the emperor.

Aurangzeb ruled as a devout Muslim, and considered himself as a religious leader as well as a political leader. He imposed the 'jijiya' tax on Hindus again, and intensified attacks on Hindus, destroying many Hindu temples, and built mosques on those very sites. "Hindu merchants were penalized by heavier duties; the provincial administrators were instructed to replace Hindu employees with Muslims; and most notoriously of all, newly built, or rebuilt temples were to be destroyed",[2]. These actions further alienated Hindus, who had been on friendly terms with the Muslims until this time. Aurangzeb also arrested and killed Teg Bahadur, the Sikh Guru, and this act angered the Sikhs as well. The Sikhs, under the leadership of Guru Gobind Singh, rebelled against Aurangzeb. Finally, the Rajputs became rebellious when Aurangzeb killed the widowed queen and prince of Marwar, a Rajput state. The most effective resistance came from the Marathas, who were led by Shivaji. More about these resistances will be covered in later chapters. All of this resistance weakened the Moghul kingdom, and Aurangzeb fought against it until he died in 1707.

After his death, his successors turned out to be ineffective and incompetent, and the kingdom was further weakened by the invasion of Nadir Shah of Persia. He ransacked Delhi for days and issued a *'fatwa'* or royal edict for '*katl-e-am*' or public massacre. For days, Delhi was engulfed with public killings and lootings. The mighty Moghul kingdom soon disintegrated, and was ripe again for foreign invasion and occupation. The British fulfilled that role and promptly colonized India.

Chapter XII
BRITISH COLONIZATION

Many historians are surprised by the fact that Muslim invaders could occupy and rule India for centuries. In contrast, historians are bewildered by the easy conquest and long colonization of India by the British. The British did not come as an invading army with sophisticated weapons, but in the beginning, they came as trading merchants, under the banner of British East India Company. India was conquered not by a large army, but by a group of traders and office clerks. Sir William Jones has stated that Bengal (India) had been like an over-ripe mango, "fallen into England's lap while he was sleeping",[1].

Even some British historians have tried to explain the easy conquest of India by the British. "What, one must ask, impelled a 150-old trading company suddenly to embark on a carrier of conquest? And how were the British so easily able to carve out a state for themselves among the powers of post-Mughal India", and "The British would often think of their conquest in India as fortuitous. It gratified a cherished conceit about the Englishman's amateurish innocence and it abbreviated the need to confront awkward questions-like how such aggression could be justified",[2].

Unlike other invaders, the British remained 'foreigners' in India, even though they stayed for close to two centuries. The differences between the Indians and the British were too widespread. When the Suez Canal opened, the British could return to England more frequently, and very few considered India as their home. "What did distinguish the British was their sense of being outsiders. Race, creed, culture and color set them glaringly apart, so did their well-developed consciousness of a natural identity"[1].

The first Europeans were the Portuguese. Vasco da Gama of Portugal arrived in India via the sea route, avoiding the hostile land of Arabs and Persians. Before the Portuguese could settle, the Dutch, British and the French arrived over the oceans as well. In 1613, Sir Thomas Roe, the

British ambassador of King James, had received a *'farman'* or royal permission for free trade in India from the Moghul emperor Jahangir. In order to win the competition among the European groups to establish more trade, the French and British fought three battles, while there was the Seven Year War raging in Europe between France and England. After the treaty in Europe, and a decisive battle in India, the British mercantile company became the major trading power. The British East India Company then settled on the banks of the Ganges in Bengal, first in Hooghly, and then in three villages, which later became known as Calcutta. Calcutta soon became a major trading post for the British in India.

During a battle between the French and the Indian ruler of Maylapur, the smaller but better trained and equipped French army was able to defeat the larger Indian army. Europeans noticed that, "A few hundred French or British soldiers, firing in volleys from a square formation could now hold off thousands of Mughal infantrymen",[1]. Also it was noted that:

> *"The superior fire power neutralized the threat of the main Indian arm, the cavalry, as it meant that a cavalry charge could be broken up well before it could reach the infantry line. These developments provided the British with great advantage over the Indian rivals and they played a significant role in their subsequent successes"*,[4].

Most Indian generals and commanders were just political appointees, so positioned for being rewarded by the rulers, and Indian soldiers were common inhabitants who were asked to fight for the rulers. The 'soldiers' were not there to defend themselves or their home. Most of them considered themselves being oppressed already, and the change of master, from Muslim to British, was of little consequence.

In 1753, the British, under the leadership of Robert Clive were able to overrun Arcot with a small contingent of British soldiers. This increased their confidence, greed and lust for power. Eventually, "Determined to extend their profits, the British in Bengal had by mid-century begun systematically abusing the right to free trade awarded to them by the emperor",[2]. In 1756, Siraj ud Dullah, the young ruler of Bengal, tried to rein in the British, who had become too powerful. Robert Clive conspired with Mir Jafar, a general in Siraj's army, offering the throne to Mir Jafar after overthrowing Siraj. In exchange, the British were promised to be paid lavishly. The British faced Siraj's army in 1757 in the Battle of Plassey. Siraj's main army, under Mir Jafar, stood by and the British routed Siraj's remaining army. This event ushered in the British foothold in India. Even today, any traitor or backstabber is called a "Mir Jaffar" in India.

Mir Jafar, in turn, became restless being a ruler by name only, and resisted the British power grab. The British promptly deposed him and placed Mir Kashim, Mir Jafar's son-in-law, as the nominal ruler of Bengal. In time, Mir Kashim also found it intolerable to be under the thumb of the British, and went to ther Moghul Emperor, Shah Alam, for help in opposing British domination. By this time, Shah Alam was a token ruler of just a small area near Delhi, and the Moghul Empire was already dying.

All Indian forces under Shah Alam faced the British in a battle at Buxar in Bihar. The British routed the Indian forces again, and extracted a '*farman*' or Royal Edict from the Mughal emperor to be the '*Diwan*' or Governor of Bihar, Orissa and Bengal, and gained the revenue collection rights in those areas. In turn, the British agreed to pay the emperor a large sum annually. This face-saving gesture pleased the Emperor, and the British became the 'de facto' ruler for the first time. As Nobel Laureate Bengali Poet Rabindra Nath Tagore wrote "the measuring rod of the merchant transformed overnight into a ruler's mace".

This process of forging temporary alliance with a ruler against another neighboring ruler by offering "protection" and gaining wealth and power in return was used by the British over and over in India. Clive had already noted that "By offering material 'protection' to Indian rulers the British could keep them dependent without arousing much popular resentment or sharing widespread protest against foreign usurpation of powers",[5]. Clive also introduced a "dual rule" or 'indirect rule', where the Indian rulers, or '*Nawabs*', remained responsible for internal administration and justice system, but the collection of revenue remained in British hands. "It was the worst of all possible dual governments; those with responsibility possessed no power, and those with power felt no responsibility",[5].

This system of 'indirect rule' profited the British handsomely, but also produced the inevitable disastrous situation. Bengal had a bad monsoon in 1769, and faced a harsh famine. The British continued to collect revenues but did nothing to help the starving people in this horrible situation. At the same time, in addition to increasing profits for the Company, individual British officials also returned to England with huge personal wealth. Even the Company directors in England were horrified that although the British profited, "they did nothing to help the starving; taking refuge behind its nominal lack of administrative responsibility",[1]. When Clive returned to England, "... he himself became one of the richest men in England almost overnight, with a fortune of 234,000 Pounds plus an annual income worth 30,000 Pounds",[4]. In describing this miserable situation, historians have noted that, "Testimony to personal fortunes is plentiful, especially amongst the condemnations and jealous countrymen of England; systematic exploitation, although harder to quantify, is inferred from numerous examples of Indian protest and is linked with the great famine of 1770, which may have killed a quarter of the Bengali population",[1].

This famine is still immortalized in literature, ballads and folk songs in Bengal. Centuries later, harsh memories of this famine aroused resentment and caused Bengalis to take a leading role in opposition of British rule. Bengali novelist Bankim Chandra Chattopadhaya wrote a poem 'Bande Mataram' or 'Homage to Mother (India)' in the novel 'Anandamath', which is based on this tragedy. 'Bande Mataram' became a battle cry for Indians who rose against the British rule. The very utterance of 'Bande Mataram' was declared an act of sedition by the British, and many freedom fighters went to jail for uttering these words alone.

After the departure of Clive, Warren Hastings, a scholar and astute administrator, became the Governor of Bengal. Later, he became the first Governor General of all British regions in India under the 'Regulating Act' passed by the British parliament. Warren Hastings turned out to be a methodical administrator, and he started to streamline the revenue collection and distribution process by appointing Collectors in every district. He also stripped the Indian Nawabs of all pretences of power, and stopped paying the annual sum negotiated by Robert Clive. He ruthlessly continued to 'annex' small states and conquer larger states by force. Most resistance to his conquests came from the Marathas, and the rulers of Bengal, Hydrabad, and Mysore. These states were already demoralized by prolong oppression of Moghul rule, and "... powerful successor states like those of Bengal Hydrabad, Pune, Mysore and Lahore, were waxing impressively beneath the vault of Mughal authority until extinguished or suborned by the expansionist ambitions of the company",[1]. Although Hastings is credited in having secured and expanded British rule in India, he was impeached for his ruthlessness when he returned to England and retired in disgrace. "Warren Hastings left Bengal in 1785, an embittered, lonely man, longing for the peerage that would never be offered to him...",[5].

Consequent British Governors General imposed massive changes in administrative and revenue collecting systems. They "reformed" some social customs that they found offensive. They also introduced an educational system replacing the existing Indian system. Lord Cornwallis replaced Warren Hastings in 1786 not only as the Governor General but also as the Commander-in-Chief. He shed all pretences of trading and concentrated on strengthening and expanding British rule. From this time on, all Governors General kept on 'annexing' and conquering states, and introducing measures to expand their domination.

In the area of politics, the British took it a solemn duty to rule over Indians. Governor General Wellesley, "was an ardent champion of this policy, and declared that 'No greater blessing can be conferred on the native inhabitants than the extension of British authority'",[4]. Using any means, particularly the process of 'subsidiary alliances', where the British would guarantee the security of Indian states in return for complete control over the governance of the state. A British 'Resident' was placed in every state to oversee the implementation of this process, and he could act immediately at the slightest 'provocation'. Using the principle of "Might is Right", the British Governor General could arbitrarily declare a *Nawab*" or an Indian ruler unfit and take over his state. Also, rulers were denied the right to adopt a son as their heir, and when they died without an heir, their kingdoms were 'annexed' by the British. After overcoming stiff resistance from the Marathas and the Sikhs, the British succeeded in dominating entire India, 'annexing' one state after another by 1850.

In the area of social reform, the British tried to rectify some Indian customs which horrified them, such as, '*Sutee*' system, where a widow would sacrifice herself by walking into the pyre of her husband, sacrifice during religious pilgrimage and festivals, and robbery and ritual murders performed by '*Thugs*' in honor of goddess '*Kali*'. Laws were passed to change these social customs, but were only marginally successful as most Hindus just ignored the laws. Moreover, due to resentment grown out of meddling in their social customs, many Indians took part in the great rebellion of 1857, which is covered in a later chapter.

The administrative system was also made efficient and effective. The unit of administration was a District, and a District Magistrate was appointed "to keep order, watch the local chiefs, and collect the revenues",[3]. This system was totally paternalistic, based on the attitude "Government knows best", and resulted in rampant official intimidation. Only the British, some in their twenties, were posted to these high positions without any preparation for understanding the social customs and culture of India. When India became independent, it inherited an administrative apparatus designed for the British occupation, but decided to maintain it. This 'top down' administrative system was not only continued in independent India, it was also expanded and strengthened through countless licensing and controlling mechanisms, which are still in practice today, stifling entrepreneurship and causing rampant corruption.

The most significant development took place in the area of education. The British did not have all the manpower to rule over all facets of the life in whole of India. They needed middle and low level Indian workers who could fulfill the tasks allocated to them by the British officials. For this purpose Indians needed to learn English, and it was decided that "...the content of higher education should be Western learning, including Science, and the language of instruction should be English",[3]. As Macaulay declared the goal of this education system was to produce a class of 'Indians in blood and color, but English in taste, in opinions, in morals and in intellect'. Many schools, such as Hindu School and Hooghly College, were established during this time. Calcutta University was established in 1857.

This educational system did produce Indians with a knowledge of the English language; even some of them could mimic some English life styles. The British patronizingly called these anglicized Indians 'Babus'. In turn, the British were called 'Sahibs" by the Indians. Even today, Indian officials in the position of power are called Sahibs. However, many Indians were intellectually ready by the rigor of studying Sanskrit to study more. They also had a 'quest for knowledge' described as 'Gyan Yoga' in *Bhagawat Gita*, one of the most important scripture of Hinduism, they did not just stop their learning just there. They also learned about the Western ideals of the Magna Charta, self rule and democracy. They read the works of Locke, Stuart Mills and Burke. In time, they became aware of the ideals of 'Liberty, Equality, and Fraternity' from the French, and 'No taxation without representation' from the American Revolution.

They came to the conclusion that 'Freedom is a birthright', as Balgangadhar Tilak, an Indian freedom fighter, claimed. All this knowledge initiated the rise of nationalism and kindled the desire for freedom. It was the educated elite who took the leadership of the freedom movement that resulted in Indian independence.

PART V
Indian Heritage through Resistance

Chapter XIII
MARATHA RESURGENCE

During the waning days of the Moghul Empire, while the British were gaining a foothold in Bengal, a new force of Marathas was emerging in south India. By 1687, Aurangzeb had conquered most of India, including the south, and moved his capital to Aurangabad for better control. These conquered states had a tendency to resist Moghul rule, and some of them were able to declare themselves to be free again. One such resisting power was the Marathas, who not only fought the Moghuls, but continued to oppose the expansion of British domination as well.

The Marathas were led by an effective guerilla fighter Shivaji. They seized some areas of Western Ghats in the south, known as *Maharastra* or 'Great Nation'. They roamed around the mountainous regions of Deccan Peninsula, attacking and harassing Moghul supply caravans. "These 'mountain rats' would wait for caravans to wend their way into hill country and then swoop down to plunder whatever they could use to strengthen their band, which soon had the arms, money, and horses to pose a formidable challenge to Muslim garrisons",[3]. Very soon, Shivaji and his band of fighters became a legend, and the common people sheltered and supported them against the Moghul army. Once Shivaji was captured, but he managed to escape and became a more effective fighting force against the Moghuls. Aurangzeb spent most of his last days fighting the Marathas, and lost many resources in battles. These military expeditions, drained his manpower and treasury, and he lost control of the far regions of his empire as well. Maratha insurgency was one of the main reasons for the Moghuls dynasty to fall.

By 1660, Shivaji was able to defeat an army of the mighty Mughols and conquer Surat. He founded a Hindu kingdom, and "He wanted 'self rule' and the full freedom to practise his own religion in the land of his birth...",[3]. Shivaji was not only a great warrior; he was also an able ruler. "Shivaji was an astonishingly gifted conqueror, as well as an excellent organizer and administrator; and a liberal and enlightened sovereign",[1].

He had an administrative council of eight ministers, with a '*Peshwa*' or prime minister, as the administrative chief. He divided his kingdom into provinces and appointed a governor in each province, and delegated local administration of villages to local councils of '*Panchayats*' or five elders. The Panchayat system of local government has been introduced India after independence, and is still in place. He set limits of tax to be paid by the farmers on the yield and not the size of their land. This eliminated the anxiety the farmers used to have when the yield was low, but the amount of taxes did not change. The generals and governors were paid, and they did not have to lean on the population for their remuneration, as was the system implemented by the Muslim rulers. These two measures eliminated much of the extortion and intimidation exerted by the state officials, and pleased the general population.

His army was well trained and disciplined. Each soldier was instructed to treat all prisoners and soldiers of defeated army with respect. He made sure that no mosque was ever destroyed by his soldiers. He made sure that the army had proper equipment. He also had a navy, which could compete with the navies of the newly arriving European nations. Moghuls, who lived in landlocked arid regions, did not realize the importance of a navy, whereas the Marathas lived near an ocean. Under his command, and according to Hindu code of conduct, his soldiers were expected to respect women and children at all times, even after defeating an enemy. "He consciously emphasized the religious aspect of his military adventures and claimed to fight for the Hindus against the Muslim rule",[2].

Shivaji died before he could complete his mission of freeing India from foreign rule. His son Shambhaji became the ruler of Maharastra. Shambhaji turned out to be a weak ruler, who did not have the talent of his father. He was captured by the Moghuls in a battle in 1689, and was hacked to death. Even after his death, the Marathas continued to fight as if they were inspired by Shivaji, as "...he bequeathed to his sons and countrymen his fierce spirit of Hindu nationalism...",[2]. Shivaji is still regarded as a national hero in India.

Shambhaji's younger brother Rajaram took refuge in the kingdom of Karnatak, and continued to fight the Moghuls. Rajaram managed to unite the Maratha governors, and chased out the Moghuls from southern part of India. After his death, his widow Tarabai continued to fight the Moghuls, and placed her son as the ruler of Marathas. After some internal strife, Shahu, son of Shambhaji became the ruler, but he was also a weak leader. He had appointed Balaji Vishwanath as his Peshwa or Prime Minister.

By this time, the actual power was being exerted by the Peshwas. Balaji managed to get the governors of Maratha kingdom to cooperate, and put it on a solid footing. After Balaji's death, his son Baji Rao became Peshwa. He "proved to be a bold warrior and an efficient strategist",[2]. He did defeat the Moghuls and seized Delhi, and declared himself as a 'Hindu Badshah' or Hindu Emperor. But he suddenly withdrew from Delhi, and concentrated on the administration of the southern part of the kingdom. This left the governors of the far provinces to emerge as 'Maharajas' or independent rulers. Once again, the Marathas could not stay united, and internal strifes emerged. Soon, the Maratha controlled region broke into four smaller principalities, led by 'Peshwas', or ministers. The four principalities were ruled by Peshwa in Poona and Gaeekwar in the south, and Scindia in Gwalior and Holkar in Indore in the north. These four principalities constituted the Maratha confederacy. The strongest one was the Peshwa in Poona, who provided leadership among them. These rulers were effective and competent. Maratha confederacy prospered, and India was poised to be ruled by Hindus again.

While the Mughols were busy fighting Marathas in the south, the Rajputs broke away from Mughol control and established smaller Hindu states in the north. Marathas continued to raid and conquer neighboring areas, and by 1750, when the British already had a foothold in east India, Marathas had conquered most of India and they reached as far east as Bengal. However, by attempting to conquer north India from the Moghuls, the Marathas neglected the threats from the rising powers of Nizam in the south and the British in the east. This mistake proved costly for them.

In 1756, when the Mughol rule was in its last dying days, and just a year before the decisive Battle of Plassey in Bengal, Ahmed Shah, an Afghan warlord invaded India. Ironically, the Moghuls asked the Marathas for help against the Afghan invasion. Anticipating an opportunity for establishing a Hindu kingdom replacing the Moghuls, the Marathas agreed to help. Marathas asked for help from the Sikhs and Rajputs in their adventure, but they stayed neutral, as they were weary of Maratha supremacy. The battle took place in 1761 in the famous battle field of Panipath, where the Marathas were decisively defeated by the invading Afghans when their long supply route from the south was cut off. The Marathas were slaughtered in large numbers, and many more were imprisoned. This ended the hope of a Hindu rule established again by the Marathas in India. Both the Afghans and Moghuls were too weak to rule all over India, and the British were able to move into this power vacuum. Many historians believe that if this battle between the Afghan invaders and Marathas had not taken place, India could be free from Muslim rule, and in turn could have also provided a successful resistance to British domination.

Even after defeat, the Marathas continued to rule over some parts of south India. They were further weakened by an internal conflict between Peshwa Raghunath Rao and Nana Faranwis, a minister of Peshwa Narayan Rao. Raghunath Rao was thrown out of the throne, and he asked the British for help to gain control again. The British did help out, but soon they dominated Raghunath Rao's kingdom, putting it under British "Protection". One after another, the Maratha principalities accepted British "Protection", and by 1820, the Maratha confederacy was completely lost to the British. "...the Marathas lacked stable organization and cohesion. By means of a series of military operations and separate treaties with the various Maratha states, the British managed to dissolve their confederation between 1800 and 1818, and the Maratha Empire crumpled",[1]. Only the Sikhs in the north and the kingdom of Mysore in the south remained to put up any credible resistance to the expansion of British domination in India.

Historians believe that the fall of the Marathas had several reasons. They were mostly warriors, and they did not have competent administrators to look after their subjects, and thus lost the support of the population. They also neglected the economic foundation of the empire, and gradually they ran out of resources to conduct the expensive military adventures. As usual, internal strife eroded the unity that was needed to defeat the mighty Moghuls and resist British expansion. Finally, in spite of some competent leaders, most were unable to inspire and lead their subjects. All these shortcomings resulted in the downfall of the Marathas.

Chapter XIV
SIKH RESISTANCE

After the fall of the Marathas, only the Sikhs posed any significant resistance to the Muslim rule and expansion of British domination in India. Under the leadership of *'Gurus'* or Spiritual Teachers in Punjab, the *'Sikhs'* or disciples began as a religious group only, but later transformed into a strong warrior group under some great rulers of a thriving Sikh kingdom.

The Sikhs were mainly from the Jat tribe in Punjab. They were inspired by the teachings of Guru Nanak, who lived from 1469 to 1539, and preached a monotheistic and egalitarian doctrine, which became the foundation of the Sikh religion. "Nanak's God was without form but pervaded by light, to be worshipped through meditation on a repetition of his name. From early on, special emphasis was placed on congregational activities, particularly singing hymns and eating together",[1]..

After Guru Nanak's death, his main disciple Angad became the next Guru, who chronicled all the teachings of Guru Nanak. He also introduced *'Gurmukhi'* or Guru's spoken words as a new language with a distinct alphabet. The next Guru was Ramardas, who spread the Sikh religion all over Punjab. Under the leadership of the next Guru Ramdas, the Sikhs established a Golden Temple in Amritsar on land offered by the Moghul Emperor Akbar.

The next Guru, Arjun, who was the son of Ramdas, collected all the documents of Sikh doctrine and compiled them into the scripture as "*Granth Sahib*". Arjun Singh was accused by Moghul emperor Jahangir of supporting his rival Amir Khusro for the throne of Moghul Empire. Jahanghir arrested Arjun and imprisoned him with many of his Sikh followers. Later Arjun was put to death by Jahangir. Until now, the Sikhs were only a religious group. When Guru Arjun was killed, the Sikhs were outraged, and turned militant or *'Khalsa'*, under the leadership of the next Guru, Hargobind. From there on, all Sikhs used *'Singh'* or lion as their last names. Gradually the Sikhs united into a strong fighting force and began to fight the Moghuls.

While in Moghul prison, Sikhs were often restricted in hand-cuffs and were not allowed to carry any weapons, cut hair or shave. To keep this memory alive, all Sikhs symbolically began to carry five items beginning with the letter 'k' in Gurmukhi language: '*Kanghi*' or comb, '*Kesh*' or hair, '*Kirpan*' or a dagger, '*Kara*' or iron bracelet symbolizing the handcuffs they had to wear in prison, and '*Kachh*' or shorts. They also covered their long hair with a turban. This tradition is still followed today. The tall and stoutly built men with colorful turbans and unshaved faces present a striking image of India. This image is often used as a symbol of modern India.

After Guru Hargobind's death, Teghbahadur became the ninth Guru of the Sikhs. He was a great warrior. By this time, the Sikhs were effectively resisting the oppressive rule of Moghul emperor Auragzeb, who ruled as a fundamentalist Muslim following the strict tenets of Islam. He imprisoned Teghbahadur and ordered him to accept Islam. When Teghbahadur refused, he was beheaded. His son, Gobind Singh (1675-1708), was the tenth and last Guru of the Sikhs. He defeated the governors appointed by the Moghuls of the north western parts of India, and established a Sikh kingdom. He was assassinated by an Afghan, and the Guru system ended.

Banda, who was a disciple of Guru Gobind, became the next Sikh leader. He turned out to be an effective and competent warrior. Under his leadership, the Sikhs spread their kingdom in northern India. After some significant victories, Banda was defeated at the end and imprisoned by the Moghuls. In 1716, he was killed in captivity.

Even after Banda's death, the Sikhs did not stop their fight against the Moghuls. Successive Sikh leaders took advantage of the dying Moghul rule, and by 1767, they had conquered most of the northern part of India. They also took advantage of the chaos created after the brutal invasion by Nadir Shah, and united into a strong army. Soon they came in conflict with the British, who were expanding their domination in India. By 1773, Sikhs ruled from Jammu in the North, to Kangra in the South, and Saharanpur in the East to Attok in the West.

In 1798, Ranjit Singh, a Sikh leader helped Jaman Shah, the ruler of Afghanistan in gaining the throne. In return, Jamal appointed Ranjit Singh as the governor of Lahore, and bestowed the title of '*Raja*' or king. Eventually, Raja Ranjit Singh became a King of the Sikhs. With the formation of this kingdom, the aspiration of the Sikhs and Hindus to rid India of Muslim rule was fulfilled. Ranjit Singh transferred the Sikh state into a strong force against the British. "...his army, trained by French and Italian generals, was a formidable force, and the while Ranjit Singh lived, even the British dared not provoke a conflict",[4].

Raja Ranjit Singh turned out not only a great military leader but he was also an able administrator. He conquered most of northern India, and became a threat to the British. Unlike the Marathas, Raja Ranjit Singh did not believe that the British could be defeated, and he kept on avoiding a war with the British through a series of treaties. He was also pragmatic, and considered that the British domination of India was inevitable. Even though he was very effective ruler and had organized a capable army, he tried to remain independent by accepting a humiliating 'treaty' in 1809. With this treaty, the kingdom of the Sikhs reduced to Punjab only, the rest of the Sikh kingdom going to British control.

Raja Ranjit Singh built a thriving kingdom, an effective administrative system and a strong army. He defeated the Afghan ruler Shah Suja, and returned with the famous diamond 'Koh-I-Noor', which was looted and taken away from the Moghuls by the Afghan invader Nadir Shah. Ranjit Singh brought unity among all Sikh factions. For his valor and compassion, he earned respect from the Sikhs, Hindus, Muslims and British as well. Under his rule, the people lived in peace and harmony. He had competent ministers in his court, including some Hindu scholars.

Raja Ranjit Singh established a fair judicial system, and he appointed competent ministers in his court, including some Hindu scholars. He also appointed European military experts to train his soldiers. His army fought many battles against the British with competence and valor.

Ranjit Singh died in 1839, and the Sikh kingdom declined soon after his death. He failed to prepare a competent heir to the throne. His army was never put under civilian control. These factors resulted in internal strife, and the kingdom broke down into smaller 'Mishle's or sections. "The death of Ranjit Singh had left the Khalsa the most powerful force in Punjabi politics. But it was muscle without a brain, for no political or military figure emerged to lead it or harness its energies",[3].

In 1845, the British tried to 'annex' the entire Sikh kingdom,. They engaged the Sikhs in a battle contravening the existing treaty. "The Sikhs fought so fiercely that the casualties on both sides were very high",[4]. However, due to weak leadership of some incompetent generals, they were defeated. In this battle, the British faced "...the most courageous and most resolute enemy that it had ever encountered in India",[2].

After the next war in 1849, which proved to be decisive, the Sikhs were completely defeated. Without a competent leader and the usual internal disunity, they were forced to sign the "Lahore Treaty". Under this humiliating treaty, the Sikh kingdom ceased to exist as an independent state. Governor General Dalhousie put the Sikh kingdom under British rule. "The second Sikh war ended the process of piecemeal conquest which Clive had begun; the British now possessed the whole of India",[3]. According to another provision of this treaty, the famous diamond "Koh-I-Noor" was handed over to the British, who promptly took it to England. This diamond is still in display in the Tower of London.

Chapter XV
REVOLTS AND REBELLION

To expand their domination in India, the British used several methods. As described in previous chapters, Clive and Hastings used the 'Dual Rule'. Governor- General Cornwallis shed all the pretences of trading and concentrated in conquering and governing these states. Governor-General Wellesley, who ruled from 1798 to 1805, introduced the 'Subsidiary Alliance' system where the Indian rulers were guaranteed 'protection' of the British from their neighbors in exchange of an annual payment to the British. In addition, the Indian rulers had to give up most of their powers and pay for stationing a garrison of British soldiers. A British 'Resident' was posted in every state to oversee this arrangement. If any real or perceived action is taken which deemed to be contrary to this arrangement, the Resident would act promptly in 'annexing' the state.

Surprisingly, most Indian rulers, such as, rulers of Hydrabad, Ayudhya, Tanjore, Karnatak, and even the Marathas accepted this humiliating treaty. Only the Rajput and Sikh rulers put up any significant resistance to these measures. In the South, Tipu Sultan, the ruler of Mysore, refused to sign this treaty, but he was killed in a battle fighting the British, and his kingdom came under the British rule. This set an example to all Indian rulers as what to expect if they resisted the British. The common people were either blissfully unaware, or to them the change of rulers, from Muslim to British, did not matter much. Unlike the Muslim rulers, the British left most of the social customs, religious rituals and cultural activities alone. The Indian people were happy to take refuge in their culture and religion.

After defeating Tipu Sultan, the British tried to defeat the Marathas. By this time, Maratha kingdom was fractured into smaller states. Lacking unity, one after another Maratha rulers were defeated in battles. After Governor-General Wellesley returned to England, this vigorous process of conquering Indian states was halted for a while.

Between the years 1806 and 1848, successive British Governors-General continued to conquer Indian states. Strong resistance to the expansion of the British Empire came from the rulers of Nepal, Marathas, Burma, Afghans, and the Sikhs. Gradually, all their kingdoms were put under the treaty of Subsidiary Alliance. It provided a face-saving pretence of power to the Indian rulers, when all the power was held by the British.

It all changed significantly when Dalhousie came as Governor-General in 1848. He ended this policy of Dual-Rule, and implemented a process of 'annexing' all Indian States for a direct rule of the British. He used three methods of 'annexing' Indian states: direct conquest in battles, deposing rulers for 'misrule', and the 'Doctrine of Lapse'. Any ruler could be arbitrarily and unilaterally accused of 'misrule' by the British, and their state could be put under direct British rule. The large kingdoms of Awudh, Hydrabad and parts of Burma were taken over by the British in this process. Many common people, not just the rulers, were alarmed by these unfair practices. Unlike the rulers, the people were passive when the Indian states were being put under British control. "The latter were not interested in political matters, but rightly saw in English policy an attempt at cultural and religious colonialism that threatened India's own civilization",[1].

In India, adopting a son as heir is very common. Under the Doctrine of Lapse, the rulers who had no son were denied the right to adopt a son as their heir, and their kingdoms were 'lapsed' under British rule. The states of Satara, Jaipur, Nagpur, Udaipur, Jhansi and Bhagat were all put under British rule using this doctrine. Nana Sahib, the adopted son of Peshwa Bali Rao, who was accepted by previous British Governors- General as a ruler, was ousted by Dalhousie. The ruling 'Rani' or Queen Lakshmibai of Jhansi was deposed as the British considered that only a son could inherit a kingdom. This measure contradicted the accepted social customs of the people of India. Finally the British managed to upset Indians by altering their social and religious customs to expand British domination. "The extremely rapid expansion of British domination –imposing administrative and judicial concepts that differed greatly from the country's ancestral traditions caused backlashes that were often violent",[1].

The British took many other measures to 'reform' many accepted social and religious practices. Governor General Bentink outlawed the practice of Sati, and Dalhousie passed a law allowing the widows to remarry. Following Macaulays proposal, English education system, with opening up a medical college replacing the Indian educational system, was introduced. . "Although these activities were hailed by educated Indians as humane and progressive, to the vast majority they seemed only the first steps in an all-out assault on Indian culture",[3].

Dalhousie also introduced a network of railway system to transport troops and raw materials. Indian farmers were forced to produce items needed for the factories in England. By this time, the industrial revolution was underway in Europe, and many raw materials, such as, cotton, jute, timber, indigo and sugar cane were needed for expanding industries. Indian weavers could not compete with the cotton mills of England, and their means of livelihood was destroyed. Frustrated and angered, both the rulers and the common people of India were ready to revolt. Historian Tammita-Delgoda describes the situation as:

"The policies of abolition and annexation greatly alarmed Indian ruling classes, many of whom were already deeply uneasy about British expansion. These deep-seated feelings of fear and unease were also shared by the majority of the ordinary people. The spread of English education, the astounding technological innovations, the unprecedented social reforms, all had a deeply disturbing effect on conservative minds. Combined with the effect of the increasing missionary activity of the times, it seemed to give the impression that Indian religion and culture itself was in danger",[3].

Between 1818 and 1856, several tribes from various parts of India revolted against the British. They were limited to local areas or groups, isolated and sporadic. The participants were no match for the trained British army with superior firepower. All were eventually defeated and put down, but the losses for the British, both in resources, lives, and prestige was enormous. The first were the Bhils, who revolted three separate times between 1818 and 1825. Jats were the next group to revolt in 1824. They were put down with the help of Gurkha soldiers. Former rulers of Sambalpur and Sitara, who were deposed under the "Doctrine of Lapse", rose against British rule in 1824. They were defeated after a prolonged bloody battle. Villagers of Kohlapur revolted against their zamindar, who collected revenues for the British. Between 1829 and 1855, the tribal groups of Santhals, Mundas and Nagas revolted and ferociously fought the British with bows and arrows. They were all finally defeated by 1856, when the British practically ruled over entire India.

During all these revolts and discontentment, the Indian soldiers in British army were loyal and disciplined, but their dissatisfaction was also rising beneath the surface. They felt unfairly treated when they were denied equal pay with the British soldiers. No Indian soldier was ever promoted to the officers' ranks. Indian soldiers did not like being deployed in far-away places, such as Burma, to fight for the British. The anger among the Indian soldiers was already mounting, ready to explode. The spark was ignited in the process of the use of a special cartridge for their rifles. The soldiers had to load these cartridges after stripping off their wrappings with their teeth. These cartridges were greased with cow and pork fat, which were prohibited under the religions of the Hindu and Moslem soldiers. Many soldiers found it a deliberate attack on their religions.

Mangal Pandey, a Hindu soldier in Bengal, fired the first shot against a British military officer in 1857. The news of this incident spread all over India and soon the soldiers in Meerut openly rebelled on May 16, 1857. They marched to Delhi, and easily captured it. They declared Bahadur Shah, an unwilling and incompetent descendent of Moghul dynasty, as the emperor. This was a symbolic act, but it followed by rebellions by soldiers in Rajputana, Bihar, Kanpur, Lucknow and Benaras. Common people, under the leadership of Nana Sahib, the heir of the Peshwas, who was denied the title, joined in with Tantia Topi and Kunwar Singh, two powerful leaders. Rani Lakshmibai, the deposed queen of Jhansi, who was not accepted as an heir because was female, attacked the British garrison. All of a sudden, practically the whole of India erupted against the British and the British hold in India was dangerously threatened.

At first, many British soldiers, along with many civilians, were killed. In Kanpur, over one thousand civilians had surrendered, but they were killed in captivity. However, most soldiers in the south remained loyal to the British. The Raja of Gwalior helped the British. In the north, the British were able to get an upper hand with the help of Sikh and Gurkha soldiers. Most people, particularly the educated elite of Bengal remained neutral. Gradually, the British succeeded in putting down the rebellion. Tantia Topi was hanged, Nana Sahib fled to Nepal, and Laksmibai died in a battle where she fought heroically to the end. She became a legend, and still today, many clubs, teams and squads for girls are named after her.

The British remembered all the atrocities of the Indians against them, particularly the women and children. They, in turn, began to retaliate and take revenge. And retaliate they did. Based on the letters written by British officers, historian Danielou has described the situation as:

"According to the letters written by British officers of the time, every day princes and ministers were tied to the mouth of cannon, in front of British officers calmingly taking tea and laughingly at the victims' contortions. This was followed by an incredible manhunt. British soldiers massacred and tortured any Indian who fell into their hands; their own servants, the villagers, sometimes the entire towns",[1].

Historian Keay describes that "...old men, women and children were sacrificed, as well as those guilty of rebellion...They were burned alive in their villages...Some of the British boasted in their letters they had spared no one and that 'nigger-chasing' was a most amusing sport"[2].

The rebellion was not a united and planned effort. It lacked coordination among participating groups, who fought on different grounds. Most leaders limited their efforts to a certain area, and many influential groups, such as the Sikhs, Gurkhas and Rajputs remained neutral, some even helped the British. The British soldiers, better trained and organized, and possessed more powerful fire power, were also fighting for their lives. All these factors led to the failure of the rebellion.

However, the effect of this rebellion was profound and far reaching. The British government realized that the governance of India could not be left to traders, who had only profit motives. In 1858, the British government took direct control of the administration. "The administration of India was controlled by the Secretary of State in London, and the policy followed; particularly by the Foreign Ministry, was dictated by European interests",[1]. On November 1, 1858, Queen Victoria issued a "Queen's Proclamation", where "The new policy was to maintain the status quo; there would be no more interference with Indian customs and religions. Nor there would be any more interference with the government of the Indian princely states",[3]. At that time, 542 Indian princely states were recognized and their rulers became known as "Maharajas" or great kings. These states remained princely until the independence of India in 1947. Queen Victoria became the "Empress of India" in 1877, and the Governor-General's position was transformed into a "Viceroy" or vice-regal.

The British civilians in India barricaded themselves into smaller "Civil Lines" in major cities, and set up garrisons in nearby "Cantonments". Whatever contact between the British and Indians that had taken place until now was seriously severed. The British remained isolated in their communities, and never became a part of the larger Indian society. In summer, many of them lived in "hill stations" established over the hills of Himalaya Mountain Ranges. They remained separated in their encloves, with their own shops, clubs and meeting places. All social contacts between the British and Indians were severed, and gradually the relationship of "rulers and ruled" developed. The Indian soldiers were barred from being trained to use cannons. Indians were not allowed to hold supervisory positions in the army or civil service. All privileges were bestowed upon the British.

The educated Indians, who were expecting the British to follow the liberal ideas they taught, and had been neutral during the rebellion, were disillusioned. "In fact, the feelings of hostility and inequality between Europeans and Indians, which had not previously existed, developed gradually, turning India into a real colony, where the Europeans enjoyed immense privileges, constituting a 'superior race'. It was this attitude that, a century later that led to the nationalist movement and independence",[1].

PART VI

Indian Heritage in Modern Age

Chapter XVI
RENAISSANCE AND REFORMATION

In the nineteenth century, when the British were consolidating their grip on India, a remarkable development in the realm of literature and religion took place in India, particularly in Bengal. This intellectual development, often called the Bengal Renaissance, blossomed into a political movement resulting in the independence of India.

This development started in Bengal, where a group of '*Bhadraloks*' or English educated elites and '*Zamindars*' or landholders took on the task of ushering in revolutionary intellectual, social and political changes. The Bhadraloks, who were usually from middle class Bengali families, and were educated both in the Indian system and in English schools. Most of them did not need to work, or were teachers and writers, and spend much of their time in intellectual discourses, publishing periodicals, and authoring books. The Zamindars, on the other hand, collected revenues from the peasants, similar to the Mansabdars during the Mughol rule, and paid a permanent amount to the British. Zamindars were mostly middle class Bengalis, who were often educated and patronized art and culture, but did not hesitate to be ruthless in exploiting peasants.

Historians have compared this movement with the European renaissance, which was followed by the age of enlightenment, industrial revolution, exploration of the new world, and establishment and exploitation of colonies. In the Bengal renaissance, a number of authors, poets, dramatists, philosophers, and novelists such as, Raja Ram Mohan Roy, Ishwar Chandra Vidyasagar, Bankim Chandra Chattopadhya, Madhusudan Datta, Dinabandhu Mitra, Rabindranath Tagore, created social and religious awareness through their writings and lectures. This was followed by religious and social reforms initiated by Abanindranath Tagore, Keshab Sen, Ramkrishna and Vivekanada. These changes ushered in a political awareness in the twentieth century that resulted in the freedom movement. This development began in Bengal, because it benefited from its geographical location, where most educational institutions with the

English system were established. The effects of this movement, often termed as the Bengal Renaissance, later spread all over India.

Rabindranath Tagore, son of Abanindranath Tagore, dominated the intellectual and artistic scene of Bengal with his multifaceted creativity. He wrote numerous novels, plays, poems, short stories, and composed a unique form of lyrics, called Rabindra Sangeet. All of his creations had some sociological, religious or political point to explore, and he single handedly raised the stature of Indian literature all around the world. For his creation of *"Gitanjali"*, a collection of poems, he was awarded the Nobel Prize for literature in 1913, the first Asian to be so honored. Later, he was also knighted by the British government, which he refused after the massacre at Jalianwala Bagh. When Rabindranath met Gandhi, he called Gandhi a *'Mahatma'*, or 'Great Soul'. Gandhi, in turn, called Rabindranath a *'Gurudev'* or 'Divine Teacher'.

In addition to great literature, a number of newspapers and periodicals were established during this period. Dramas were created and performed to reflect social issues, and *'Sabhas'* or associations were formed to discuss and initiate religious and social reforms. Several factors have been attributed to these developments: English education introduced liberal philosophical ideas, particularly democratic ideas, and new scientific and technological advancements found ready acceptance among the educated elites. Leisure provided by the Zamindari system and the growth of a rich merchant class provided an opportunity for patronage and financial support for such intellectual activities.

As stated before, this movement was initiated and nurtured by the educated elite, and the common peasantry remained mostly untouched. This produced a greater gulf between the classes. Even most Muslims remained aloof, resulting in more division along religious lines among the population. This division proved to be fatal and is regarded as the main cause of the partition of India.

After centuries of occupation and oppression, religious and social reformers found that the Vedic culture had degenerated and was mired in thoughtless rituals and moral degradation. Several customs, such as polygamy, caste system, the Sati system, and forced extravagance during social and religious activities were found to be deplorable by these intellectuals. Abuse by the upper class of the society, exploitation by the rich and powerful had become common. Consumption of alcohol, and keeping professional entertainers as concubines, and excessive promiscuity had become the style of some of the aristocrats, called *'Babus'* by the British. The Babus did everything to ape British life style, and loved to hobnob with the British.

Christian missionaries, with active patronage of the British, tried hard to exploit these sentiments to spread Christianity. Many English-educated Indians were schooled in Christian missionary schools, and were influenced with the Christian doctrine. "Many actually left the Hindu fold to become Christians and they looked upon the English people and the English way of life as their ideal which Indians must reach if they were ever to attain manhood. The Englishman's way of life was the supreme goal of their ambition.",[3]. Notable intellectuals, such as Parbati Charan Banerjee, K.C. Bannerjee, Dr. L.M. Mukherjee, Dr. Goodeve Chakraborty, and eminent Bengali poet Madhusudan Datta, converted to Christianity.

At this time, Raja Ram Mohan Roy, a Bengali aristocrat, studied the teachings of Islam, Christianity, and Hindu religions. He found some aspects of Hinduism as was practised at that time, such as the Sati system and idol worship to be abhorrent. "He preached an abstract monotheism, and was against the cult of images. He recommended the recitation of Veda texts, but was open to all castes, favored inter- caste marriage, forbidden by Hindu law, and the remarriage of widows",[1].

Raja Ram Mohan Roy also considered that Indians should study only in schools following the English system. He wanted Indians to stop studying Indian languages, scriptures and philosophy. He petitioned William Bentinck, who was the Governor-General of India from 1828 to 1835, to ban the Sati system, and allow the English system of education only. Ram Mohan succeeded in some of his efforts, and the Sati system was abolished by law. Later, he appealed to Lord Amherst, the next Governor-General to fund English system schools only. With his efforts, Hindu College or Presidency College, and General Assembly Institution or Scottish Church College were established.

Raja Ram Mohan Roy also formed *Bramho Sabha*, a social activists' group, in 1828. "In practice, his cultural innovations were designed to make Brahman ideas more relevant for urban Bengalis who worked alongside Europeans in Calcutta and who formed the beginnings of what would become India's middle class",[2]. Bramho Sabha attracted many educated Indians, and under the leadership of Henry Dirozio, an Englishman born in India and a teacher at Hindu College, they formed the elite group called "Young Bengal". This group studied the works of European scholars and discussed the various aspects of social reforms.

Another scholar and reformer, Ishwar Chandra Vidyasagar was born in a poor Brahmin family in 1820. He studied in Sanskrit College, and excelled in Indian philosophy. He wrote many books, and helped establish Bethune College. He also tried to introduce social reforms, and with his effort, education among women spread considerably, and an act was passed to allow widows to remarry. He wrote books for the teaching of Bengali and Sanskrit languages which are still used in India.

In 1843, Debendra Nath Tagore, an eminent philosopher, established the *Bramho Samaj* or Bramho Society, along the lines of Bramho Sabha. "Bramho Samaj became the refuge of the more intellectual and more spirited youths, who wanted to break away from Hindu faith but did not like to join Christianity",[3]. Gradually, the educated youth found more reasons to remain Hindu, but accept the reformed ideals. Keshab Chandra Sen, another leader of Bramha Samaj, split with Debendra Nath. "He then formed a new sect, called the Bramha Samaj of India. He extolled the practice of ecstatic community chanting and singing called sankirtana. The worship of idols was replaced, however, by the adoration of religious leaders",[1]. He formed similar organizations in other parts of India as well. These organizations continued to stress social reforms, and attracted many followers. One such follower, Mahadev Ranade, established the *Prathana Samaj*, or prayer society, in Gujarat in 1867. At the same time, Swami Dayananda Saraswati, another reformer from Gujarat, established the *Arya Samaj*. Arya Samaj, with other religious reforms, undertook the task of missionary activity and reconverted the Indians who had converted to Christianity and Islam into Hinduism. The missionary task was and is still rare among Hindus.

These organizations continued to stress social reforms, and attracted many followers. Similarly, Sir Syed Ahmad introduced social reforms among the Moslems as well, and established Aligarh Anglo Muslim College for Muslims. He was knighted for his help to the British during the great rebellion of 1857.

In northern India, Bharatendu Harishchandra resisted total Anglicization, and revived Brahmanism. He developed the use of the Hindi language in the press, books and journals. He founded *Kashi Dharma Sabha* in 1860, and stressed the importance of Hindu customs of image worship and *Bhakti* or devotion to God. In Maharastra, Bal Gangadhar Tilak developed a radical approach of reform, and called for 'Swara'j or Self Rule as a birthright. He is considered to be the first leader to oppose British rule. He revived pride in Hinduism, particularly in the heroic deeds of Shivaji.

The census of 1871 provided stimulus for social groups and castes to unite and form Sabhas or associations. In southern India, Virasalingam founded Rajamundri Social Reform Association in 1892. Gokhale founded the Servants of India Society to foster education among girls and depressed classes. Jyotiva Phule founded the Satyashodhak Samaj in 1873 to challenge the domination of upper class.

At this time, Ramkrishna, born in 1833, emerged as a saint and mystic in Bengal. The emergence of Ramkrishna from obscurity was the work of Keshab Sen. Ramkrishna could describe the complex philosophy and teachings of Vedas and Upanishads in very simple terms, and he stressed the universality of Hinduism. "Ramkrishna inspired middle class individuals who sought to encompass the manifold diversity of their cultural environment, transcending the West's materialism and Christianity, and incorporating Islam into a larger cultural essence in the idiom of Upanishads",[2]. Gradually, the educated youths, such as Vivekananda, Bramhanada, Sivananda, and Saradananda, who had accepted Bramho Dharma turned back to Hinduism. "That was the beginning of great trek back to Hinduism",[3].

Vivekanada was to become the most famous religious leader of this era. His original name was Narendra Nath Dutta and he was born in 1863. He had an English education and studied the Koran, as well as the Bible. In 1833, he was invited to represent Hinduism to the Parliament of Religions held in Chicago, where "..the force of his personality and his eloquence created a strong impression",[1]. Vivekananda later formed a religious order called Ramkrishna Mission to spread the teachings of Ramkrishna. Vivekanda worked tirelessly to reform Hinduism by incorporating values in the light of Western ideas.

Two more powerful Hindu leaders, Sasadhar Tarkachuramani and Krishnananda Swami, helped Hinduism to be accepted again. At this time, Bankim Chandra Chattopadhya, a former Indian Civil Srrvice officer, who had quit his position of Deputy Magistrate protesting British injustices, wrote *Ananda Math*, a novel based on the Hindu rebellion against Muslims, with the song "*Bande Mataram*" or 'Homage to Mother (India)'. Bande Mataram became a rallying cry for the rebellious Indians who led the struggle for freedom from British rule.

Many historians have wondered about the fact that in spite of centuries' long Muslim and Christian rule, Hinduism remained so vibrant and relevant. In most societies, the people tend to accept the religion of the ruling power. Even when the educated elite were turning away from Hinduism, the vast unlettered mass of the people of India remained firm in their Hindu faith and tradition. When the Moslems, who were considered outsiders by the Hindus, wanted to destroy Hindu establishments, their attacks only put the Hindus on their mettle. A galaxy of spiritual leaders, such as Nanak, Ramananda, Meera Bai, Tulsi Das, Kabir and Chaitanya Deva, emerged to reassert Hindu faith.

The most formidable challenge to Hinduism came from Buddhism. Buddha was born in India, and his teachings found acceptance among many Indians. However, after Buddha's death, Kumarilla Bhatta and Sankaracharya reestablished Hinduism by their sheer eloquence and intellectual power. In the classic tradition of inclusiveness and adaptability of Hinduism, Buddha was accepted as an incarnation of the Supreme Divinity of Vishnu of the Hindus. Buddhism almost vanished from India, with the exception of the eastern part of Bengal. East Bengal remained Buddhists, and when Muslim domination spread to that region, most people converted to Islam. It was this region that was split from Bengal to form East Pakistan, later to secede Pakistan and become Bangladesh.

Chapter XVII
RISE OF NATIONALISM

The changes brought through reforms undertaken during the late nineteenth century did not confine in the cultural, social and religious sector, but eventually spilled over to the political area as well. With cultural awakening and scrutiny of social conditions, questions were raised about the consequences of British rule.

Several other factors also contributed to this awareness. Between 1780's and 1860's, India changed from an exporter of processed goods, such as textiles, minerals, gold and silver, to become the main export market for British goods, particularly textile from cotton mills of England. The Indian textile industry completely collapsed and India became an exporter of raw materials, such as, cotton, indigo, timber, oil seeds, jute and tea, for an industrialized England. These developments resulted in economic hardships among Indians, resulting in resentment and anger.

The British had taken total control of the land revenue system in 1792, which eventually resulted in 'permanent settlements'. In this system, settlements were awarded to create permanent political allies and establish economic stability. The local tax collectors or 'Mansabdars' who were to collect revenues from people, suddenly became 'Zamindars', or permanent land owners. This zamindari system created a layer of rich, ruthless and aristocratic group in society, which provided protection for the British against popular unrest. Zamindari system also fit the early modern state form; zamindars became virtual autocratic rulers of their land. Zamindars were regarded as mere stooges of the British, and much resentment among the populace grew against them. Many atrocities were committed by zamindars against the peasants, particularly during bad crop years. Due to all these developments, the gulf between the rulers and the ruled widened even more.

The British had built many canals and an extensive railway system to transport goods. By 1900, India had the fifth largest railway system in the world. This system enabled Indians to travel to other regions, which provided a unifying factor. At the turn of the century, the British needed cash to wage wars, expand territories, and undertake public works to move goods. All these factors added to the need to collect revenue by any means, often resulting in rebellion, as it happened in the "Indigo Uprising" in 1860.

India also provided indentured labors for the British colonies in the Far and Middle East, Caribbean and Africa. These laborers differed from slaves in name only. They worked in harsh conditions in cane and cotton fields, mines and ranches. Tales of their woes eventually reached their families in India who became disillusioned and resentful.

For a long time, Indian soldiers in the British Indian army have been loyal and disciplined. Under British command, they were deployed to grab and secure British interests in Asia and Africa at the cost of Indian tax payers. No Indian was allowed to become an officer, even after over a million Indians fought effectively and died in battlefield under the command of British officers in the First World War. This rule was changed only in 1935. By that time, resentment within the army had developed considerably.

The British, after long and uninterrupted rule in India, had become overconfident and arrogant. They believed that it as their right to rule over the Indians. "They endeavored to secure the economic interests of empire, establish secure border, and provide a government of limited responsibilities",[1]. They became insensitive to the feelings of Indians, and imposed arbitrary changes in legal and administrative areas. Imposition of the British-styled judiciary system replacing existing Indian laws and practices, and the structure of the administrative system caused resentment even among the educated elites.

The Indian Civil Service, a system of selecting and placing senior administrative positions, was designed mainly to keep Indians away. One had to stay at least two years at a University in England before taking the selecting examination. This barred many Indians from trying for administrative positions. During the rule of Governor-General Duffrin, the administrative posts were divided into three categories: imperial, provincial and subordinate. The first two categories were set aside only for the British. Under the Act of 1793, no Indian could earn a salary higher than eight hundred rupees, which was only a fraction paid to British officers. This limitation had not been changed even after almost a century. All educated Indians, no matter how competent or skilled, could only achieve subordinate positions. The highest position that an Indian could achieve was that of a Deputy Magistrate.

Many Indians, who went to England for higher studies, came back with liberal and democratic ideas. They hoped to have a say in the administration. But as their hopes were frustrated, they turned to open rebellion. As dissatisfaction grew, a group of Indians, occupying relatively higher posts in administration, gathered in 1885 in Bombay at the instigation of A. O. Hume, an Englishman. This gathering, under the leadership of a Bengali lawyer W. C. Banerjea, formed an association known as the Indian National Congress. It was hoped, that this body "...if properly managed, would constitute an irrefutable answer to the assertion that India was incapable of having representative institutions",[1].

The Indian National Congress, later known as Congress, limited its efforts just to appealing for representation in policy-making stages. It showed loyalty to the British rule, and affirmed its faith in the sense of justice of the British. After repeated rebuffs during the next two decades, its attitude changed into suspicion, and eventually it pursued a policy of constitutional agitation. Congress demanded, and often succeeded, in bringing in some changes in favor of Indians. However, their actions were limited to petitions and discussions only. Some leaders in Congress became disillusioned with the Congress' policy of petitions and its ineffectiveness. Under the leadership of Arobindo Ghosh and Bipin Pal of Bengal, Bal Gangadhar Tilak of Maharastra, and Lajpat Rai of Punjab, they became fiery nationalists and demanded '*Swarajya*' or self rule.

In the nineties, two natural disasters produced further dissatisfaction among Indians. In 1896, the Monsoon, that ushers in rainfall which is essential for agriculture, failed, and in 1899, a disastrous famine followed. Also, a catastrophic bubonic plague happened in India at this time. These two calamities resulted in a decade of extreme suffering to the masses, and the poor handling of the situation by the British administration conditions became critical. Wasteful military adventures in Assam and Manipur regions in India to secure interests of British tea planters and imposition of a five percent levy on imported cotton goods "...became a dramatic symbol of imperial government's concern for British manufacturer at the cost Indian industry",[2].

In 1899, George Curzon came to India as the Viceroy. He was convinced that "...efficient administration by benevolent autocratic rulers best served the country",[2]. He streamlined the bloated bureaucracy, and appointed a commission to study the problems of university education. No Indian was appointed in this commission. This action alienated more Indian scholars, who until now believed in the sense of justice of the British.

All these developments resulted in strong nationalist feelings among some Indians, who were led by Surendranath Banerjee. He was a brilliant scholar and fiercely nationalistic. He was an officer in the Indian Civil Service, but quit to establish the Indian Association in 1876. Its objectives were to unify all sectors of Indian people, promote friendly bonds between the Hindus and Muslims, and spread education among the masses to form a strong body of public opinion opposed to British rule[3]. In 1883, when Ilbert Bill was passed to allow Indian to try Europeans, it was protested vehemently by the British, and was promptly rescinded. This fact confirmed the notion among the Indians that they were not going to be treated fairly by the British, and they lost faith in the British Judicial system. In 1883, Surendranath organized an Indian National Conference in Calcutta, and in 1886, the Indian Association merged with Congress. He became the primary leader of the Indian nationalist movement.

The final spark that ignited widespread resistance to his policies came in 1905, when Curzon tried to divide Bengal into two provinces. He wanted to weaken the nationalistic movement of Bengal by dividing it into Bihari and Oriya dominated Western part and Muslim majority Eastern part, thus cutting off the power base of Hindu nationalists, who were the main source of nationalism. The "...decision to partition Bengal into a Muslim majority province and a Hindu majority province was seen by Indians leaders as a sinister move to perpetuate divide-and-rule policies by creating a split between two Bengali communities that shared a common language and culture",[3]. This partition was strongly opposed by Bengalis. The educated middle class in Bengal rose under the leadership of Surendra Nath Banerjee, who galvanized not only Bengalis against Curzon's attempt to divide Bengal, but inspired nationalists all over India. "Nationalists across the country took up Bengali's cause, appalled by British arrogance, contempt for public opinion, and what appeared as blatant tactics to divide and rule",[2].

On October 17, 1905, the day Bengal was divided, the whole of Bengal, if not whole India was seething with anger and erupted in huge protest. Universal fasting and general strike were observed in Bengal. The British responded by taking severe measures: beating protesters and arresting leaders. These measures only resulted in more agitation, and some Bengali youths took up arms in protest.

This armed movement targeted British officers and several attempts were made to bomb British establishments. Many participants of this armed movement, such as, Barin Ghosh, Prafulla Chaki, Satyen Bose, Khudiram Bose and Kanai Dutta, were hanged, imprisoned in Andaman or exiled in Burma. Bhagat Singh was hanged and Chandrashekhar Azad died in a shoot out with the police. Balgangadhar Tilak and Lajpat Rai were also jailed for exciting feelings of disloyalty towards the British government, and Arobindo Ghosh took refuge in Pondicherry, a French settlement. These oppressive measures only heightened opposition to British rule. As a result, nationalism took a firm hold in India, and a mass movement for an independence erupted.

Chapter XVIII
STRUGGLE FOR SELF RULE

Nationalism in India rose during the early years of the twentieth century, and it climaxed in the next two decades due to various incidents and developments. In 1909, the long awaited India Council Act was enacted, which allowed Indians to be included into provincial legislatures only, but not at the centre. Indian members were to be elected by members of local public bodies: chambers of commerce, universities, landholders, and jute and tea planters. Continuing the policy of 'divide and rule', special seats were reserved for the Muslims. This proved to sow the seeds of division along the basis of religion, which later resulted in the disastrous partition of India. Some moderates in the Congress embraced these reforms, but most were disappointed, and continued to demand more substantial reforms for self-rule.

In 1911, Viceroy Hardinge, arranged a spectacle and pageantry of an "Imperial Durbar" in Delhi for Emperor George V. Too much was spent for this extravaganza, and only the elite and princes who were deemed to be friendly to the British were invited. Many Indians, who were crying out for self rule, found this event meaningless and wasteful. Also, at this time, the British moved the capital from Calcutta to Delhi, mainly to be away from the uprising that was convulsing Bengal.

When the First World War broke out, the Indian Army was dragged in to fight under British command. Enormous loans were raised in India for this war, and over one million Indian soldiers took part. These soldiers had a huge number of casualties. It was hoped that the British would reward them by granting more opportunities for self rule and grant dominion status, similar to the status granted to other 'white' British colonies, such as Australia and Canada. Their hopes were dashed when the British refused to grant any degree of self-rule, and instead imposed more oppressive measures, and clamping down any dissent.

When the Turkish Empire was dismembered after the First World War, and the defeated Sultan of Turkey was deposed, the Muslims in India felt humiliated and betrayed as the Sultan was regarded as the *Khalif* or the spiritual leader by many in a Muslim sect. These resentments resulted in the "*Kihlafat Movement*", mainly led by Muslim leaders all over the world, including India. Indian Muslims were also resentful when the division of Bengal was rescinded in 1909, as they were hoping to get a province in India with a Muslim majority. Until this time, most Muslims had remained loyal to the British, and did not join the Nationalist Movement that had began all over India.

In 1914, Mohandas Gandhi, born in Gujarat in 1869, but educated as a barrister in England, came back to India. He had led Indians living in South Africa to oppose apartheid policies of the government through peaceful means of non-cooperation. At first, he put an effort into helping the British in the War, but later took up the cause of disenchanted Indians against the British. He also changed his appearance from an anglicized lawyer to an Indian monk, half naked and wearing only a rough home spun cloth. "Gandhi's look of a Biblical prophet won the trust of the Indian masses and impressed the Westerners",[1].

Under the leadership and instigation of Sir Syed Ahmad, many Muslims left Congress, which he thought to be Hindu dominated, and established the All India Muslim League in 1906. However, Mohammed Ali Jinnah, a Muslim barrister, remained members of both the Congress and the Muslim League. The British continued to address the Muslims as a separate group, and helped "create a sense of self-identity among the Muslim community as a whole by guaranteeing that the Muslims would achieve substantial gains politically and economically if they could forge a 'national identity' as a counterpoise to the Congress",[4].

In 1919, the Rowlett Act was passed by the officials of the British India Government, but not by the elected members of the Executive Council, and severe measures were introduced to combat the rising aspirations for self-rule. This Act enabled the government to arrest and detain any persons merely on suspicion of sedition and keep imprisoned without a trial by the courts. This Act antagonized even some moderates, who were hoping for some reforms for self- rule.

The passage of the India Act of 1919 provided for a legislative assembly at the centre, and legislative councils in provinces, that included some Indian members. Some departments of the provincial government were to be administered by ministers appointed by the governors, and the rest was to remain under the direct control of the governors. This dual government or 'Diarchy' was introduced with the formation of separate electorates for Hindus, Muslims, Christians, Europeans and Anglo-Indians. Only a handful of moderates in Congress welcomed this development, but it was strongly opposed by the rest. In protest, some moderates left the Congress and formed a Liberal Party in 1919. Congress reacted to this Act through a compromised resolution by Balgangadhar Tilak 'to accept it with reservation and disappointment', rejecting calls for full acceptance by Gandhi. Chittaranjan Das, a prominent lawyer and aristocratic leader from Bengal wanted it to be rejected outright.

Chittaranjan Das opposed the British rule and led the nationalist movement with pragmatism and worked tirelessly to unite all factions of society. "He rejected the idea that India develop along Western lines and he advanced a vision of India's uniqueness based on India's distinctive, all-inclusive national culture",[2]. He worked tirelessly to bring Hindus and Muslims together, and was respected by both groups.

Armed with the Rowlett Act, the British clamped down on any dissent with more oppression. This climaxed in the Amritsar massacre, where a peaceful crowd had gathered in Jalianwala Bagh Park. The local commander of the garrison, Colonel Dyer, took his Gurkha soldiers, and fired on the peaceful crowd after trapping the exit. Three hundred and seventy unarmed people were killed, and over one thousand were wounded. Dyer defended his actions and was received in England as a conquering hero and awarded a purse of three thousand sterling pounds.

The reaction to this massacre was swift and severe all over India. Indians, who have been cooperating with the British, openly opposed the British rule. Bengali poet and Nobel laureate Rabindranath Tagore rejected his Knighthood, and Gandhi began a non-violent movement "*Satyagraha*", or 'Quest for Truth'. Gandhi became the undisputed leader of India, particularly after the untimely deaths of Balgangadhar Tilak in 1920 and Chittaranjan Das in 1925. Gandhi took over the Congress replacing Gopal Krishna Gokhale and Surendranath Banerjee as the prominent leaders.

The watershed year for the British rule in India proved to be 1919. The Amritsar Massacre, disappointment over 'reforms' and *Khilafat* issue galvanized all sectors of Indians against the British. Gandhi began one of his peaceful non cooperation movements, and asked for rejecting and boycotting all British sponsored institutions, such as local bodies, schools and colleges, and imported goods. This was termed the "*Swadeshi*" or

'Own Nation' movement. Mohammad Ali Jinnah opposed Gandhi's call as it was not based on purely religious issues, and left the Congress.

In the next two decades, Gandhi led three great campaigns of civil disobedience. In 1920, the civil disobedience movement was observed throughout India, and the freedom movement transferred from a small group of elites to the ordinary people. However, when a group of Indians stormed a police station and killed several policemen, Gandhi called off the movement in 1922. This disappointed many other Indian leaders, such as, Chittaranjan Das and Motilal Nehru, who formed a *"Swarajya"* or Self-rule Party.

In 1930, Gandhi led another movement to oppose the "Salt Act", where the Indians were not allowed to produce salt. This caught the imagination of the masses and they followed Gandhi's lead and broke law by collecting salt from the sea. The British reacted brutally, arresting over 60 000 and killing 103 people in 1930 alone.

To 'divide and rule', the British responded with some concessions to pacify the moderates, and with arrests and imprisonment of the others. Several commissions to 'Study' the situation and round table conferences to negotiate with Indians took place. Although all such measures resulted in failure, finally the British did realize that they could not hold on to India anymore. In 1935, the Government of India Act abolished 'Diarchy' and extended autonomy to provincial legislatures. A provincial election, with an extended but fractured electorate in communal groups, was also called. These developments energized the Congress, and "In a stunning triumph, winning 758 of 1505 seats in 1937 formed governments in seven provinces",[3]. The Muslim League failed miserably, and could not form government in any province. The Muslim League became deeply frustrated and communal feelings among Muslims deepened.

By 1935, the British power was in retreat. The outbreak of the Second World War was "the final deciding event in the story of Indian independence."[3]. Faced with mass civil disobedience, armed uprisings, and the Second World War, the British slowly and grudgingly agreed to negotiate with Indian leaders for some concessions for self-rule and even some representation in the Executive Council of India.

PART VII

Indian Heritage in Independent India

Chapter XIX
MASS MOVEMENT

Under the leadership of Gandhi, the Indian National Congress continued to aim for a dominion status of India. At the same time, Subhas Chandra Bose and Jawahar Lal Nehru, two young leaders, wanted nothing less than a complete and explicit break from British Empire and demanded full independence for India. Nehru introduced a resolution for "complete national independence" in the Annual Session of Congress in 1927. However, this resolution was opposed by Gandhi, who considered that Indians were not ready for independence, and the resolution was finally rejected. Subhas Chandra Bose continued his effort to pass a resolution for complete independence, and in 1929 it was passed in the Annual Session of Congress at Lahore. This was the first time a pronouncement for full independence was made, and this declaration caused the awakening of a new spirit in the nation.

Subhas Chandra Bose was a brilliant scholar and leader, who left the Indian Civil Service, commenting that "it is neither Indian, nor Civil, nor Service". He advocated for the independence of India with any means, including armed struggle. This was too much for Gandhi. He declared Nehru as his successor, and forced Subhas Bose to resign from his position of President of Congress in 1939. Subhas Bose established the Forward Bloc, a group within Congress. However, for his extremist views, this group was banned in 1940 by the British, and he was put under house arrest. In a daring act, he escaped and reached Germany where he established the 'Azad Hind' or Free India Radio. In 1943, he went to Japan, and led the Indian soldiers who were taken prisoner by the Japanese Army, and formed the 'Azad Hind Fauz' or Indian National Army (INA). He also established a Provisional Indian National Government in exile.. The Indian National Army, along with the Japanese Army, marched towards India, and reached Kohima and Imphal in Assam, India. However, the INA was stopped when Japan was defeated and the logistical and material support from Japan ended. Subhas Bose is said to have died in a plane crash, but as his body has never been found, several conspiracy theories are still actively discussed. He is regarded a national hero in India.

When the Second World War broke out, without consulting any Indian leader, Viceroy Linlithgow declared India to be at war. He suspended any talks of democratic reforms and deployed over two million Indian soldiers in Africa and East Asia against the Axis Forces. These unilateral actions infuriated the Congress leaders, and they "...offered to support the War if India was given immediate self-rule",[3]. When this demand was not met, all Congress provincial ministries resigned in protest. In contrast, the Muslim League offered full support and cooperation to the British. This left the political arena to the Muslim league alone, and they continued to gain more prominence.

As the Muslim League claimed to represent all Muslims, and continued to gain strength, some Hindus were alarmed. Many joined Hindu Mahasabha, an organization established in 1906 by Madan Mohan Malviya to advance the cause of Hindus. Hindu Mahasabha gradually became active in politics, and under the leadership of Shyama Prasad Mukherjee, accused the Congress of appeasing the Muslims. Shyama Prasad opposed Nehru's effort to reach out to the Muslims while preaching secularism at the same time. In 1939, the Muslim League declared 'Islam in Danger' and called all Muslims to join in '*Jihad*' or Holy War against the Hindus.

The communal rift grew wider, and by 1940, the Muslim League was demanding a separate territory for Muslims. Jinnah became the undisputed leader of the Muslim League and he passed a resolution for the creation of 'Pakistan' or 'Holy Land', "...stating that, 'Mussalmans (Muslims) are a nation according to any definition of a nation and they must have their homelands, their territory, and their state'",[2]. Another rift to Indian unity came from the '*Dalits*' or low caste Hindus under the leadership of Bhim Rao Ambedkar, also known as Baba Saheb Ambedkar. The Sikhs, not to be ignored, organized under the leadership of Master Tara Singh and demanded Sikh representation in any talks with the British. The British were only too happy to exploit these acrimonies.

In 1941, Winston Churchill, the British Prime Minister, and Roosevelt, the President of United States, declared that they respected "...the right of all peoples to choose the form of government", but Churchill insisted that this declaration did not apply to India. However, under pressure from Roosevelt, Churchill announced in March 1942 that Stafford

Cripps, a Labor member of the War Cabinet, was going to India with a 'radically new scheme of constitutional reform'. Cripps' proposal included a new Indian Union status to 'ensure racial and religious rights of the minorities, and no part of India will be forced to join the Union'. This proposal was rejected by the Congress as they considered it a blow to national unity and also rejected by the Muslim League as it did not accept the formation of a separate Muslim State.

With the failure of the Cripps' Mission, disillusioned Congress leaders rallied under Gandhi, who demanded an immediate end of British rule in India. In August 1942, Congress launched a mass civil disobedience movement, later to be known as the 'Quit India' movement. Viceroy Linlithgow responded by arresting and imprisoning most Congress leaders with over sixty thousand followers. Protest rallies were organized all over India, but Muslim League denounced this movement as a rebellion, and the Communist Party of India, under instructions from Moscow, condemned this movement as well.

With Congress leaders in jail, Jinnah consolidated his stature, and continued to demand a home for the Muslims. At this time, Chakravarti Rajgopalchari, a Congress leader from the south, who was not jailed for his opposition to the Quit India movement, negotiated with Jinnah, and accepted the notion of a separate settlement for Muslims. This was the first time any Congress leader accepted the notion of separatism, and opened talks with Jinnah as an equal negotiating partner. When Gandhi, who was in jail, was informed of these talks, he decided to open talks with Jinnah as well. Jinnah finally got his wish to begin talks for a separate territory for Muslims.

Unnerved by these developments, the British finally realized that their days in India were numbered. Facing the mass civil disobedience movement, Viceroy Wavell was convinced that it was necessary to undertake some constitutional reforms in India. He called an election in September 1945, so that an Interim Government for '...early realization of full self-government in India', could be formed. This election took place in the winter of 1945/1946, and both the Congress and Muslim League did better than in the last election. Congress gained majority in eight out of eleven provinces, but the Muslim League won only in two out of four Muslim majority provinces.

Viceroy Wavell also released all Congress leaders from Jail in August 1945, and called a conference in Simla to negotiate a plan. He proposed a new Executive Council with representatives from the Congress, the Muslim League, Sikhs, and 'Dalits' or Lower Castes. His proposal was rejected by Congress as it claimed to represent all Indians, and the Muslim League rejected it because it did not grant a separate state for the Muslims.

When the Second World War was over, the Labor party came to power with Clement Atlee as the Prime Minister. Unlike Churchill, he was open to the idea of Indian Self-Rule. At this time, two significant incidents took place in India. A trial for three captured officers of the Indian National Army, Shah Nawaz Khan, Captain Sehgal, and Gurbax Singh Dhillon, a Muslim, a Hindu and a Sikh, began in August 1945. Both the Forward Bloc and Congress utilized this trial to raise anti-British sentiments. Congress, under the leadership of Nehru, presented a remarkable argument defending these officers. The British realized the explosive nature of the situation, and the trial ended with light sentences. In 1946, naval units in Bombay protested poor living conditions and racial discrimination and staged a mutiny. According to Abul Kalam Azad, an eminent Congress leader, "...this was the first time since 1857 that a section of Defense Forces had openly rebelled against the British",[1].

In 1946, a three member Cabinet Mission came to India with a proposal that, '...the elected provincial representatives to the constituent assembly would divide into three sections. One section would be composed of Hindu majority provinces, the second of Muslim majority provinces in the northwest, and the third of Muslim majority in the northeast. Each of these groups would draw up its own constitution'. Congress debated over this proposal and accepted it with some hesitation, as it divided India into three sections based on religious grounds. The Muslim League remained silent, pondering a response. Viceroy Wavell went ahead and installed Congress ministries, even when Muslim League had not accepted the Cabinet proposal. In a news conference, Nehru, the new President of Congress, was asked if Congress accepted the Cabinet proposal in totality, he answered that his party was, '...completely unfettered by any agreements and free to meet all situations as they arise'. This statement from Nehru infuriated Jinnah, and he abandoned any idea of a compromise, and hardened his demand for a separate 'Pakistan'. To force his demands, Jinnah called a day of 'Direct Action' in India on August 16, to '...organize the Muslims for the coming struggle to be launched as and when necessary'.

In Bengal, the Muslim League ministry of Hussain Surawardy called a Day for Direct Action as well. This action unleashed a horrible communal holocaust in Bengal, particularly in Calcutta. Mob killing and looting took place for four days, resulting in over four thousand dead and thousands more wounded. Only when the Gurkha soldiers moved in, were the killings gradually stopped. These killings triggered riots in other places, such as, in the Noakhali District of Bengal, and in Bihar and Punjab as well.

Horrified with these developments, Prime Minister Atlee declared on February 20, 1947, that 'His Majesty's Government wishes to make it clear that it is their definite intention to take necessary steps to effect the transfer of power into responsible Indian hands by a date not later than June 1948'[1]. A unified India was out of question by this time. It is ironic that the resistance to British rule mainly started in opposition of the partition of Bengal in 1905, but it ended with a plan to partition Bengal. Keeping up with the historical tradition, Indians failed to unite again, even for a common goal of Independence.

Chapter XX
PARTITION AND INDEPENDENCE

As stated in the previous chapter, Viceroy Wavell persuaded Nehru to form an interim government, even without the participation of Jinnah, the leader of the Muslim League. The new government consisted of Nehru as Vice Chairman of Viceroy's Executive Council with Ballabhvai Patel, Rajendra Prasad, Rajagopalchari, Asif Ali, John Mathai, Baldev Singh, Shafat Ahmed Khan, Syed Ali Zaheer, C.V. Bhaba, and Sarat Chandra Bose as members. Sarat Bose was later replaced by a person representing the lower caste, by this time known as "Scheduled Caste". Feeling isolated, Jinnah agreed to join the interim government, but "...he had no desire to offer genuine cooperation; his intention, to the contrary, was to work from within the interim government to wreck it",[3]. During this time, communal riots continued to take place all over northern India. In order to break the impasse, and to expedite the transfer of power, Prime Minister Atlee of Great Britain replaced Wavell with Louis Mountbatten as the Viceroy of India.

After meeting the Indian leaders, Mountbatten realized that keeping India intact was out of question at that time. He proposed a plan for partitioning India along communal lines: one part composed of the Muslim majority provinces of the North West Frontier Province, Sind, Baluchistan, and the Muslim majority part of Punjab in the west, and with the Muslim majority part of Bengal and Sylhet district of Assam, to form independent Pakistan, and the rest of India to form independent India. Further, both these parts to be granted dominion status. The princely states were free to join Pakistan or India, or could remain unattached. This plan was accepted by the Congress leaders with much reservation, but enthusiastically accepted by the Muslim League. Gandhi was strongly opposed to it, and he offered Jinnah the Prime Ministership of an undivided India. It was considered impractical and was outright rejected by Jinnah and even by Nehru and Patel as well. In Bengal, Shyamaprasad Mukherjee and Sarat Bose tried to confer in vain with Najimuddin, the Muslim

League leader in Bengal, to avoid the partitioning of Bengal. They even tried to keep undivided Bengal as an independent state. All such efforts came to an end when the Muslim leaders in Bengal could not guarantee that they will not join Pakistan.

Mountbatten did not have much time to undertake the immense task of dividing the Army, government bureaucracy, and all public assets. All government employees were given a choice to accept positions in Pakistan or remain in India. Due to a disciplined army, and a well trained civil service, the transition took place relatively smoothly. The same was not the case in the general population, particularly in Punjab and Bengal. The consequences of partition in these two provinces were severe and catastrophic.

People had to be uprooted from their homes, causing immense problems. Ugly violence flared up all over, and millions were chased out their homes, creating millions of refugees. They brought back horror stories of slaughter and mass murder, causing retaliation. "Over half the Muslims stayed in India, on the other hand, Hindus in Pakistan were despoiled, massacred, deprived of their civil rights and protection",[1]. Neither Mountbatten nor Nehru was prepared for this terrible development.

Mountbatten appointed two boundary commissions presided over by Cyril Radcliffe to prepare a detailed plan for the partition of Punjab and Bengal. He completed this complicated task in a extremely short time. He flew back to England after submitting the plan to Mountbatten. Mountbatten decided not to publish the plan until after the Independence of Pakistan and India. Indian leaders, and the general public, did not know the details, and could not prepare for the partition. Moreover, when Mountbatten was asked by a reporter about the day of independence, he casually replied that the transfer of power would take place on August 15, 1947, well ahead of the deadline set by Prime Minister Atlee.

At midnight of August 14, 1947, Nehru became the first Prime Minister of Independent India, and Mountbatten accepted to remain as the Governor- General. In his inaugural speech from the Red Fort in Delhi on that day, Nehru declared, 'At the stroke of midnight, when the world sleeps, India will awake to life and freedom'. He also likened this journey as a 'tryst with destiny'. Gandhi, however, disappointed with the partition, did not join in any festivities, declaring *Yeh azadi jhutha hai*', or "This freedom is false". He stayed away from politics from there on, and put all his effort in quelling communal feelings. Mahatma Gandhi, as he was known all over the world, was assassinated in 1948 by Nathuram Godse, who opposed Gandhi's overtures towards Muslims as blatant appeasement.

The euphoria of independence was, however, short lived, as the monumental task of tackling ugly communalism begun. The infant nation had to deal with immense social, economic and political problems created by long neglect and the consequences of an abrupt partition. It was the first time India had emerged as a single political entity to be ruled by Indians. India gained the status of nationhood, but lacked a sense of nationality. Historian Lytton Strachey (1888-1932) described India as "a name which we give to a great region including a multitude of different countries...the first and most essential thing to learn about India is that there is not, and never was as India, or any country of India, possessing, according to any European ideas, any sort of unity, physical, political, social or religious". "In 1947, a free India emerged as a new state in the international state system, but it was neither a state proper, connecting a well-defined territorial entity, ...nor a state in the accepted sense of 'nation-state'"[3]. The first task was, therefore, to build a nation.

The creation of Pakistan was more of a mistake, as "It gave the Middle East an unstable state –Pakistan—without economic, industrial, or cultural superstructures",[1]. Indians who left Pakistan were mostly educated professionals, whereas Muslims leaving India were mostly peasant laborers. Also, the death of Jinnah in 1950 deprived Pakistan of a competent and charismatic leader during its infancy. Geographically, Pakistan was an oddity, with two parts, West Pakistan and East Pakistan, separated by thousands of miles. The two parts had nothing in common except religion. They were different in all other aspects, such as, race, culture, and customs. Most importantly, they spoke different languages. History later proved that religion only was not enough to keep them together. The two parts separated after a bloody upheaval. Pakistan is now regarded as a "failed state", mostly ruled by Generals of the army, and dominated by the clergy. Civilian Prime Ministers are unceremoniously toppled, and regularly hanged, exiled or assassinated.

The issue of the native states was handled by Ballabhbhai Patel. He managed to get most native states, over 500 of them, to integrate with India. In exchange, the princely rulers were offered annual sums of money as 'privy purses', and were allowed to keep their titles. Some rulers were offered governorships. In a few cases, such as Hydrabad and Junagarh, the army was deployed for "police action", resulting in their integration with India. "This, by any reckoning, was a stupendous achievement. It had been brought about by wisdom, foresight, hard work, and not a little intrigue",[2]. Only the accession of Kashmir is still not resolved, and has remained a source of constant conflict between Pakistan and India, and has caused the rise of terrorism.

The first task, Indian leaders decided, was to prepare a Constitution of their own to fulfill the goal of "...promoting nation unity and facilitate progressive social change",[2]. In addition to these goals, the Constitution had to establish the mechanism for a functioning government. To undertake this task, a Constituent Assembly was created from the elected members of the 1946 election. This Constituent Assembly had 300 members, who were educated elites, and were elected by only fourteen percent of a selected population group, and therefore did not reflect the general population of India. Jawahar Lal Nehru set the parameters of the Constitution of India, which was later included into the Preamble, for a nation that is an

"...independent sovereign republic, guaranteeing citizens justice, social, economic and political; equality of states opportunity; and before the law; freedom of thought, expression, belief, faith, worship, vocation, association and action, subject to law and public morality...", all this while assuring that, *"...adequate safeguards shall be provided for minorities, backward and tribal areas, and depressed and other backward classes"*.

The other influential leaders in framing the constitution were Bhim Rao Ambedkar, Ballavbhai Patel and Rajendra Prasad. Ambedkar foresaw the provisions for preserving the rights of the minorities. Most of the detailed work of the Constitution was done by Patel. He worked at mediating between warring groups, removing conflicts among them. Rajendra Prasad, a brilliant scholar and lawyer, preserved the dignity of the process, and managed the inclusion of fundamental values of India along the Vedic life style. Although India is officially secular, effects of Hinduism is present in many areas of the constitution. For example, the national motto of India is *"Satyameva Jayate"*, or 'Truth Alone Triumphs', a direct quote from *Katha Upanishad*, Chapter II, *"Sloka"* or Verse 2.2.

The Indian Constitution is the largest constitution in the world, as it had to fulfill three tasks: nation building, framing the working of a nation, and undoing existing and deplorable social customs. It borrowed ideas from the constitutions of the United States, France, Russia and the common laws of Britain. It is federal in nature, ensuring a strong central government against regional disparities. The central government is structured with a President as the head of state and symbol of the nation, and a Prime Minister heading the executive branch of the government. Parliament is composed of two houses, Lok Sabha, with members elected directly through universal suffrage, and Rajya Sabha, where some members are nominated and others elected by Vidhan Sabhas, or provincial legislative assemblies. The judiciary is independent of the executive and legislative branches.

The Indian Constitution brought in national revolution focusing on democracy and liberty, whereas social revolution stressed secularity, equality and justice. In addition, as Patel declared, 'We are building a nation and we are laying the foundation of One Nation'. The new Constitution of India was adopted in 1949, and on January 26, 1950, a "Sovereign, Democratic Republic of India" was established. It was a significant achievement. "Moral vision, political skill, and legal acumen were all brought together the framing of the Indian Constitution",[2].

Chapter XXI
NEHRU-GANDHI "DYNASTY"

According to the new Constitution of The Republic of India, the first general election took place in 1952, and it became a grand spectacle for democracy. India was acclaimed as the "Largest Democracy in the World". Over 173 million voters voted for 4000 seats. As most voters were illiterate, symbols were used to denote candidates in addition to their names and party affiliations. Congress scored a sweeping victory, but several delegates were elected from some non-Congress parties, such as, from the leftist Communist and Kisan Majdoor Parties, and from the right Swatantra and Janasangha Parties. No party elected enough members to become the official opposition. In spite of that, leaders such as Acharya Kripalani, Lal Manohar Lohia, Shyamaprasad Mukherjee and Tridib Chowdhury, managed to offer significant opposition to the government.

With this sweeping victory, Nehru gained almost absolute control both of the government and the Congress party as well. The death of Ballabhbhai Patel in 1950 had already removed any serious challenge to his leadership. With no significant opposition, Nehru dominated all aspects of India until his death in 1964.

Nehru faced a country with a depleted treasury, tattered economy, and with acute shortage of resources. He pursued socialist policies for economic development, , "Nehru wanted the State to introduce, encourage, and oversee the development of large scale and small scale enterprises, the former publicly owned and the latter cooperatively owned",[3]. At first, he tried to introduce land reform by imposing a ceiling on land holdings, and thus eliminating large land owners, known as 'Jagirdars' and 'Zamindars'. However, with limited surplus land, this step failed to provide enough land to the landless farm laborers and poor farmers.

Nehru also launched a coordinated and ambitious development project known as the "Five Year Plan" in 1951. Construction of huge dams and the building of heavy industries such as steel plants were undertaken in this plan. These measures did improve the irrigation system somewhat, and produced much needed electricity, and the steel plants improved the industrial output. However, in the Second Five Year Plan, the agrarian sector was mainly neglected, and this resulted in acute shortage of food in 1957. India was forced to accept the wholesale import of grains from the United States. By the time the Third Five Year Plan was introduced, Nehru's socialistic plan was in full implementation, and "...it did not promote any capitalist enterprise in India",[3], as government controls through licences thwarted entrepreneur spirit. According to the Industries Act of 1951, and the Companies Act of 1956, government control on industries was absolute. "The controls and restrictions that it imposed on the economy stifled and suffocated growth, engendering red tape and inefficiency on an enormous scale",[4].

In foreign affairs, Nehru pursued a "Non-Aligned" policy by not favoring the Western or the Communist blocs. However, in the height of Cold War, his habit of 'lecturing' and accusing Western nations for colonialism and their policies of capitalism did not endear him to the United States and much of Western Europe. The Defence Treaty signed by Pakistan and United States in 1952, and Nehru's closer alliance with the Soviet Union further widened the rift between India and the United States. In turn, the United States followed a policy of "tilting" towards Pakistan. During his trip to Soviet Russia and Communist China he was received warmly, and he formed a close alignment with those communist countries. He was gravely disillusioned when China attacked India in 1962, and he "...felt duped and humiliated",[4].

Domestically, Nehru faced challenges from various linguistic groups to reorganize provinces, now called States, on a linguistic basis. He resisted these demands as he considered that it would raise regionalism, but finally succumbed to the pressure. In 1952, Andhra Pradesh was formed for Telegu speaking people. Later, Tamil Nadu for Tamils, Kerala for Malayalis, and Karnataka for Kannada speaking people were formed. In 1960, Gujarat for Gujratis, Maharastra for Marathis was formed as well. In 1966, Harayana for Hindi speaking, and Punjab for Punjabis were formed.

Nehru's most controversial act was the passage of the Hindu Code Bill. The passage of this Bill ignited the strongest opposition in India. This Bill defined and established a new code for the social customs of the Hindus, mainly for marriages and succession arrangements. Many prominent Hindus, such as, Rajendra Prasad, the President of India, Swami Karapatriji of Ram Rajya Party, and Nalini Ranjan Sengupta, President of Shastra Dharma Prachar Sabha, considered it unwanted interference of government and a direct assault on their religious and social traditions. No such Act was proposed for the Muslims. After much controversy, this Act, Hindu Marriage and Hindu Succession Acts were subsequently passed. Further, the Untouchability Act was passed to set aside special quotas for government jobs and admission to universities for the 'Dalits' or the Scheduled Castes, as the people of "lower" castes were known. These steps further intensified resentment among other groups in India.

After Nehru's death, his daughter, Indira Gandhi, but no relation to Mahatma Gandhi, became the compromise Prime Minister, after a brief Prime Ministership of Lal Bahadur Shastri. During Shastri's tenure, Hindi was declared as the national language of India, which caused much opposition and agitation among non-Hindi segments of India, particularly in Tamil Nadu in the south. Indira Gandhi engaged in a bitter power struggle within the Congress, and split the party. Her faction was known as the Congress (Indira) Party. She continued her father's socialistic policies, and was forced to ask for food aid from the United States, when an acute shortage of food took place in 1966.

Under Indira Gandhi's rule, the "Green Revolution" was implemented in India where farmers were given new funds and technologies, including a new variety of grain seeds developed by Indian scientists from Mexican models. This resulted in an increase in grain production, and India became self-sufficient in food production for the first time.

In 1970, the Awami League party from East Pakistan won majority in the general election in Pakistan. Awami League leader, Sheikh Mujib, was poised to become the Prime Minister of the whole of Pakistan. However, the rulers in West Pakistan rejected the verdict of the people, and sent the army to arrest Sheikh Mujib. The Bengalis from East Pakistan rebelled, and many refugees poured into India. Indira Gandhi sent troops to help the Bengalis, and soon East Pakistan seceded from Pakistan and the new nation of Bangladesh was formed. For these decisive and bold actions, Indira Gandhi became immensely popular.

Gradually, Indira Gandhi turned erratic and autocratic. When her election was declared invalid for electoral irregularities by the High Court, she imposed the State of Emergency and suspended the Constitution on June 26, 1975, curtailing civil rights of all citizens. Facing tremendous resistance, she lifted the Emergency in 1977. In this election, the Congress party lost. A coalition government of Janata and Jana Sangha parties was formed with Morarji Desai as the first non-Congress Prime Minister. Desai was a former Congressman and a minister in Nehru's cabinet, but had left Congress protesting the autocratic rule of Indira Gandhi.

In the 1980 election, Indira Gandhi won again, but she faced a new challenge. The Sikhs, under the banner of Akali Dal, wanted to have a separate State for the Sikhs. An extremist group, under the leadership of Jarnail Singh Brindanwale, demanded a separate independent homeland for the Sikhs, or Khalistan. "Anyone who opposed him was assassinated and by the end of 1984, his followers had murdered hundreds of moderate Sikhs and Hindus",[4]. When some terrorists amassed a huge quantity of weapons and holed up in the Golden Temple in Amritsar, the holiest place of Sikhs, Indira Gandhi sent in troops to remove them. After much destruction of the holy temple, and death on both sides, the army managed to end the siege. This action angered many Sikhs, and Indira Gandhi was assassinated by her own Sikh bodyguards in 1984. After her death, her son, Rajiv Gandhi, a professional pilot, was selected by the Congress (Indira) Party as the Prime Minister.

Rajiv Gandhi won an election in 1985, mainly with a sympathy vote. As the Prime Minister, he moved away slightly from Socialist policies, and presented a budget which "...sought to remove some of the controls and checks,...trade regime was liberalized, with duties reduced on a variety of imports and incentives provided for exports",[1]. These changes opened up a floodgate of individual entrepreneurship and brought in an unprecedented boom in the economy.

After this spectacular economic success, Rajiv Gandhi faced problems on many other fronts. He became very unpopular for his decision to send troops to the Sri Lanka in response to pleas from Sri Lankan government to help them quell insurgency from the Liberation Tigers of Tamil Elam (LTTE). Over one thousand Indian soldiers died in this conflict, and it was called by the press as "India's Vietnam".

At this time, Shah Bano, a divorced Muslim woman, went to court to seek alimony from her affluent husband, who had denied it. The Supreme Court ruled in favor of her, but this decision was opposed by fundamentalist Muslims, particularly by the clergy, who considered it to be an intrusion into Muslim Personal Laws. Many Muslim leaders blamed Rajiv for this development. They also granted a 'fatwa' or verdict against the ruling, and raised the cry of "Islam in Danger". To pacify them, Rajiv passed the Muslim Woman Bill in 1986 to recognize the supremacy of Muslim Personal Laws in matters of divorce. Hindu leaders objected to this special treatment for the Muslims, and pointed out that the Hindu Code Bill, which was passed before, did alter Hindu Personal Laws. Rajiv managed to anger both the Muslims and the Hindus at the same time.

Rajiv was also accused of accepting bribes from Bofors, a Swedish arm manufacturer. By this time, the Congress Party had weakened considerably, and lost the election in 1989. During the next election campaign, Rajiv Gandhi was assassinated by a female suicide bomber who opposed his policies towards the LTTE. The long rule of the Congress Party, and more significantly, rule of the Nehru-Gandhi "dynasty", seemed to have ended with his death. However, according to the political pundits, Rajiv's widow, Sonia Gandhi, is the 'real power' behind the ruling coalition at the present time. Rahul Gandhi, Rajiv and Soniya's son, has turned out to be a savvy politician and an effective campaighner, and many consider him being groomed to be the future Prime Minister of India. Maybe, the Nehru-Gandhi "Dynasty" has not ended after all.

Chapter XXII
RISE OF REGIONALISM

After the 1989 election, a coalition of disparate parties, such as, Janata Dal, formerly known as the Janata Party and Bharatiya Janata Party (BJP), formerly known as Jana Sangha, joined forces under the leadership of the former finance minister of Rajiv Gandhi's cabinet, Viswanath Pratap Singh. V. P. Singh, as he was commonly known, defeated Congress and formed a coalition government. This was the beginning of a series of unstable coalition governments. All national parties had lost ground and regional parties managed to prop up larger parties to form coalition governments, exerting huge and disproportional paybacks in return.

Singh tried to implement the controversial recommendations of the Mandal Commission, which recommended that more seats in universities and government services should be reserved for the Scheduled Castes, and 27% additional seats should reserved for unspecified Other Backward Class (OBC). Over three thousand seven hundred groups, comprising of 53% of the total population, claimed to belong to OBC, and demanded the privileges allocated to the Scheduled Castes. This move was opposed by many, particularly by the BJP, and the coalition government of Singh collapsed. But, the damage was done, and small, caste-based regional parties sprang up all over India, causing political uncertainties, and fragmenting Indian society on caste lines. After this 'Mandalization', India changed forever for the worse. In all further elections, coalition of smaller parties formed unstable and unreliable governments. These coalition governments had to keep the partners in line, which restrained the governments from taking bold and necessary, but unpopular decisions.

A greater communal disaster happened in 1980 at a mosque called Babri Masjid in the city of Ayodhya that shook India to its core. This centuries old mosque is said to have been built by Babur in 1528, after razing a Hindu temple on a site to be known by Hindus as '*Ramjanmabhoomi*' or the birth place of Lord Rama. By 1986, several Hindu organizations, such as Vishwa Hindu Parisad (VHP) and Rastriya Swamsevak Sangh (RSS), campaigned for a Hindu temple to be rebuilt on the site of Babri Masid which had been abandoned for over four hundred years, and was in a state of ruin.

Sudddenly, Babri Masjid became a symbol of Muslim solidarity, and Muslims demanded that no temple should be built there. The BJP used this opportunity to harness the Hindu emotions, and thrived to champion the Hindu cause, or *'Hidutwa'*. BJP leader Lal Krishna Adwani launched a symbolic *'Rath Jatra'* or chariot journey on a remodeled car evoking an ancient Hindu tradition from Somenath Temple in Gujarat which was looted by Muhamad Ghazni, a Moslem invader, in the eleventh century, to Ayodhya. Even though Adwani was arrested, he gained much prominence.

Finally, frustrated by inaction, Hindu 'Kar Seva' or volunteers of VHP, stormed and demolished Babri Masjid in 1992. Liberals and Hindu intellectuals were horrified with this action of bigotry and religious fanaticism, and many expressed dismay over the perceived end of secularism and tolerance in India. Prime Minister Narasima Rao dissolved all BJP State governments, banned VHP and RSS, and arrested many BJP leaders. However, these actions did not placate Hindu-Muslim tensions, and riots broke out all over India, killing thousands.

Dispute over the site lingered in the judicial system, without a clear outcome. The VHP staged several religious ceremonies at the site to keep the claim alive. However, the issue did not get resolved. After one such religious ceremony in 2004, as some *'Kar Seva'* members were returning to their homes in Gujarat, their train stopped in a railway station called Godhra. While the train was at this station, a confrontation broke out between the Hindu volunteers and Muslim vendors at the station. Suddenly, the train caught fire trapping the Hindu volunteers, and fifty eight of them were killed. In retaliation, violence erupted all over Gujarat, particularly in the big cities. Thousands of Muslims were killed in a few days. Narendra Modi, the Chief Minister of Gujarat, justified the killings as retribution. These acts horrified many, both in and outside India, and dire predictions were made about India's future. However, "...these dire predictions had not come to pass. In theory, if less assuredly in practice, India remains a secular state. The rule of law is not what it might be, but the rule of the central government still runs over most India",[1].

At the same time, relations between India and Pakistan continued to worsen, mainly on the Kashmir issue. Border conflicts continue to occur, draining resources and manpower from both nations. "Pakistan was actively involved in training and financing the dissidents in Punjab and Kashmir",[3]. In 1989, Kashmiri insurgents kidnapped the daughter of a Muslim cabinet Minister, and demanded the release of fellow insurgents who were awaiting trials. V. P. Singh's government was not prepared for this development, and caved in and met their demands. This emboldened the insurgents and *Jihadist* terrorism rose dramatically, and communal feelings in India hardened. Weak coalition governments could not take decisive actions, and Indian society continued to fragment along communal lines.

The situation worsened more dramatically, and Kashmiri '*Jihadis*' or Islamic insurgents raised havoc attacking Hindus in Kashmir, known as Pandits. Thousands of them, or over half of all Hindus, left Kashmir, and became refugees in their own country. Tensions grew further when India in 1998 and Pakistan in 1999 carried out successive nuclear tests and became nuclear powers.

Ironically, during all these religious and social upheavals, the economy in India improved dramatically. In 1991, Narasima Rao of Congress became Prime Minister, and he faced staggering annual debt payments and depleted foreign revenues. To meet the requirements of the International Monetary Fund loans, Finance Minister Dr. Manmohan Singh presented a budget to simplify and rationalize taxes, abolish tariffs and reduce government subsidies for private businesses. Thus India, "...took part in a worldwide transition in which national economies were increasingly integrated into a global economic system",[2]. These steps were resisted by business groups in India, who were not ready to give up the protection of tariffs. The labor unions, as directed by the Communist Party, also objected to this liberalization of economy and did not like the rise of "Capitalism". The BJP also objected, fearing that this liberation would, "...end economic self sufficiency and the influx of foreign goods would make India lose its cultural values",[2]. It was strange that both the left and right resisted these bold but necessary initiatives.

These policies liberated India from the failed policies of Nehruvian socialism, and unleashed a flood of new private businesses. India had an unprecedented economic growth, as the GDP rose over six percent annually. The size of the middle class also increased dramatically with increased domestic consumer consumption. Free from government restrictions, new Indian entrepreneurs, ushered in a boom in business adventures. At the same time, the highly skilled and English speaking professionals joined the Information Technology (IT) revolution. However, the short- sighted politicians, fearing loss of "vote banks" and campaign donors, did not let Manmohan Singh undertake all the necessary steps for more liberalization, and government control and restrictions through licences continued to stifle the economy.

Gradually, the BJP morphed into a Hindu conservative party under the leadership of Lal Krishna Adwani. BJP gained popularity among upper-class Hindus, who were disenchanted by the implementation of recommendations of the Mandal commission. After communal tensions among extremist Muslim and Hindus broke out, Adwani stressed the cause of '*Hindutwa*' or Hindu ethos. At the same time, without a strong national leader, the Congress Party kept on losing ground.

In 1998, the Bharatiya Janata Party (BJP) formed a government with Atal Behari Bajpayee, a veteran parliamentarian, as the Prime Minister. His right- leaning government focused on a strong defence and anti-terrorism measures. He also stressed the development of infrastructure and increased energy production, and further liberalized the economy. Funding on education and health care also increased during his rule.

To improve relationships with Pakistan, Atal Behari Bajpayee visited Pakistan and met Nawaj Sharif, the Prime Minister of Pakistan. For a while, relations seemed to thaw out between the two countries. But India discovered in 1999 that Pakistani troops and Islamic militants had entered India at Khargil, a remote section in northern India near the Pakistani border. India was caught unprepared, but Bajpayee swiftly dispatched the army instead of dithering and negotiating with Pakistan as it had been done so many times before after similar incursions. After much loss of life, the Indian army managed to evict the Pakistani invaders. As Islamic militants and Jihadists continue to grow and the army gained more prominence in Pakistan, Pakistani-supported Islamic terrorists' attacks continued to take place not only in Kashmir, but all over India.

Congress leaders tried in vain to stem the rise of BJP, but it continued to lose popularity. In desperation, they begged Sonia Gandhi, the widow of Rajiv Gandhi who was born in Italy, to take the leadership of Congress in 1998. Sonia did not agree at first, but relented in the end and took control of the party. She turned out to be a formidable campaigner, and in the election of 2004, Congress formed a government, cobbling a coalition of 'socialist' and 'secular' parties, who opposed the BJP for its radical views. BJP raised the issue of Sonia's 'foreignness', as she was not born in India, but Sonia countered by nominating an erudite scholar and astute economist, Dr. Manmohan Singh as the Prime Minister. Although he had never won an election, he was the architect of the economic liberalization of the nineties, and was respected throughout India as an honest person and skilled economist, a rarity among politicians.

In spite of these challenges, the Indian economy continued to grow, and within a decade India became a formidable economic power in the world. "India is entering the twenty-first century as a dynamic, creative country with a palpable spirit of change in the air, a sense of confidence, and no shortage of intellectually gifted people who have the ability, given a supportive environment, to remake every aspect of the country",[3].

PART VIII

INDIAN HERITAGE: SOCIAL & CULTURAL INSTITUTIONS

Chapter XXIII
DHARMA: A WAY OF LIFE

According to many Indian scholars, such as, Balgangadhar Tilak, Dyanand Saraswati, Sarvapalli Radhakrishnan, Debendranath Tagore, and Upendramohan Sengupta, the very expression "Hindu Religion", is a misnomer. When the Greek invaders reached India, they mispronounced the Sanskrit name for River Sindhu, and called it Indus. Centuries later, the Islamic invaders described the people of India as 'Hindu', describing the people living beyond the river Indu. When the British colonized India, they called all the rituals, customs, beliefs, and dogmas that did not belong to Islam and Christianity as "Hindu Religion". Indian scholars resent a term evolving from mispronounced terms imposed by invaders and colonizers. Moreover, this "religion" neither originated in the Indus Valley, nor did its followers live there exclusively.

Stressing the uniqueness of Hinduism, it has been described by both Indian and Western scholars, as being more than a religion. "Hinduism is not a religion, in the general meaning of the word. In Hinduism, there are no prophets who have fixed once and for all the 'truths' that must be believed or unalterable rules of conduct common for all. Hinduism is a philosophy, a way of thinking, which penetrates and coordinates all aspects of life and seeks to harmonize it with an infinitely diversified world whose fundamental causes are beyond the grasp of mankind",[3]. Also, "Let's say it right away, there are no Hindus. This word was invented by European colonizers to designate people which lived in the valley of the Indus",[5].

Further, "Hinduism is, however,... a religion without a unitary doctrine, revelation or textual authority. Its most noticeable attributes are its mythological richness, which can be traced back to the Vedic religion or before...Thus, paradoxically, among the wide range of Indic beliefs, stories, ideas and customs, there are some recurring tenets which hold the same significance as notions of sacrifice and salvation...",[6]. Sarvapalli Radhakrishnan, an eminent Indian philosopher, wrote, "Hinduism is more a way of life than a form of thought. While it gives absolute liberty in the world of thought, it enjoins a strict code of practice",[7]

The term used in ancient scriptures to describe the features of Hinduism is *"Dharma"*, which is a derivative of the Sanskrit root verb *"Dhri"*, meaning "that which holds", or "to sustain", and Dharma literally means "...the essential nature that one holds". "It is so called on account of its capacity for the sustenance of the world...There is no English word that conveys all the meanings of Dharma, but 'duty', 'law', 'obligation', 'proper action', and 'right behavior' have been used by translators",[4] and is natural and present in all humans. Dharma is, "...an untranslatable Sanskrit term that is, nonetheless, cheerfully defined as an unitalicized entry in many English dictionaries. The Chambers Twentieth Dictionary describes it as 'the righteousness that underlies the law...no one word translation 'faith', 'religion', 'law', can convey the full range of meaning implicit in the term",[11].

Richard Lannoy, in his book *The Speaking Tree*, describes Dharma in nine different ways in different contexts: moral law, spiritual order, sacred law, righteousness, and "the totality of social, ethical, and spiritual harmony". Andar Hussain Khan describes Dharma as "That by which we live". This notion that Dharma is "a way of life" is most widely accepted. Sarvapalli Radhakrishnan, the second President of India, and an erudite scholar and philosopher, stated about Dharma that, "it is not an idea but a power, not an intellectual proposition but a conviction",[8].

In order to make Dharma more understandable, it has been used with some prefixes, such as *"Hindu Dharma"* or the Dharma of the Hindus, *"Sanatan Dharma"* or the eternal Dharma, *"Shastra Dharma"* or the Dharma based on 'Shastras' or the ancient scriptures, and *"Arya Dharma"* or the Dharma of the Aryas. Most concepts of Dharma are detailed in scriptures, namely, *Vedas, Upanishads* and *Puranas*. "The Vedas are more a record than an interpretation of religious experience. While their authority is final,...the interpretations are bound to change...Hinduism is bound not by creed but by a quest, not by a common belief but by a common search for truth",[7].

There are some recurring tenets of Dharma. One of them is that there are four aspirations of all human, and they are: *'Artha'* or seeking prosperity, *'Kama'* or seeking physical pleasure, and *'Moksa'* or liberation from the cycle of birth, death and rebirth. Every living being has *'Atman'* or Soul, which is Divine, and a part of the Great Soul or *"Paramatman"*.

The human soul goes through the cycle of births and rebirths until it re-unites with the Great Soul, or achieves '*Moksha*'. "...life is a cycle of re-births, from which there can ultimately be an escape (Moksha), dependent upon the performance in each lifetime of the proper duties (Dharma) of one's calling",[6]. This concept confirms the immortality and transmigration of souls.

Upanishads, also known as ''*Vedanta*' or 'End of Vedas', explain three main processes of achieving Moksha: '*Jhana*' or spiritual wisdom, '*Bhakti*' or devotion, and '*Karma*' or actions "regulated by the conception of duties or debts which one has to discharge",[8]. 'Jnana' refers to real-ization of spiritual and metaphysical concepts through contemplation and meditation, and have been achieved by scholars and reformers, gurus and spiritual leaders, known as '*Rishis*' or sages. 'Bhakti' is devotion to Para-matma, represented by Deities, through rituals, mainly consisting of of-ferings and singing of hymns or '*Stutis*' in Sanskrit and '*Bhajans*' in more present Indian languages". Throughout centuries, great personalities, lyricists and poets, such as, Sankaracharya and Vabhavuti, Vedavyas and Valmiki, Tulsidas and Mirabai, Surdas and Jayadev, Chaitanya and Ram-prasad, have created hymns for devotees to find solace.

The majority of Hindus believe that man is reborn in happy or un-happy conditions according to their works and actions or '*Karma*'. Therefore, the suffering a man endures is simply the result of his actions or '*Karmaphala*'. This belief, "...provide a potent sanction against evil-doing, or at least against man's infringing the ethical norms of his society, for this leads to inevitable suffering, while righteous conduct brings hap-piness to the next life",[1]. More importantly, *Moksha* can be achieved through righteous conduct. This belief not only stresses the importance of conduct, but also sets norms of ethical conducts, and explains the ques-tion of human suffering.

In the epic *Mahabharata*, there is a section called *Bhagawat Gita*, which teaches that one has a duty to sustain and promote progress of so-ciety. "The *Bhagawat Gita* (Song of the Lord), may be considered the most typical expression of Hinduism as a whole and an authoritative man-ual...",[1]. *Gita* implies an active way of life, and stresses the fact that all actions according to Dharma are to be fulfilled without any consideration to their consequences. The devotee serves God by fulfilling his duties as a loyal servant, and his actions are the only criterion of true worship.

Attributes of a man, as defined in Dharma and described in Chapter

16 of *Bhagwat Gita* are as follows: charity, self-control, performance of '*Yagna*' (fire rituals), study of scriptures, austerity and straightforwardness. Further, non-violence, truthfulness, absence of anger, renunciation, peacefulness, aversion to fault finding, compassion towards all beings, non-covetousness, gentleness, and modesty are also cited. Finally, brilliance, forgiveness, fortitude, purity, absence of hatred, and absence of arrogance, are also cited as the attributes. These attributes are in Sanskrit, and the translations are provided by Prabha Duneja in her book '*The Holy Geeta*",[3].

Upendramohan Sengupta, the founder of Shastra Dharma Prachar Sabha, has emphasized that '*Karmaphala*' can be overturned through effort or '*Purusakar*', mainly by righteous actions and devotion. He has also cited some unique features of Shastra Dharma, such as, Contradiction (*Maya*), Consequences of Action (*Karmaphala*), Rebirth (*Punarjanma*), Initial Action (*Prarabhda*), Caste (*Jati*), Company (*Sanga*), Duty (*Kartabya*), Being (*Jiva*), Humility (*Vinay*), Dependence on God (*Paratantra*), Own Initiative (*Paratantra*), and Truth (*Satya*),[9].

Righteous actions and fulfilling one's duties are stressed in the '*Puranas*' or 'Ancient Narrations'. There are eighteen such Puranas, which narrate actions and behaviors of various rulers and sages, gods and demons, heroes and common people, emphasizing the importance of actions. Sanskrit epics, such as, *Ramayana* created by Valmiki, and *Mahabharata* created by Vedavyas, describe the importance of fulfilling of the duties and the results of one's actions in poetic forms. These epics have been translated into almost all Indian languages, and are recited and read in millions of households and by groups of devotees.

The Vedas and the Upanishads, Smritis and Puranas, which are regarded as the foundations of Dharma, remain unchanged, but their interpretations by different scholars, such as, Sankara, Ramanuja, Madhava and Ramkrishna, may differ. In a few instances, they are even contradictory. But, all these differing interpretations are equally accepted and respected. "Among the Hindus, there was a greater tendency towards incorporation",[6]. From time to time, in regular frequency, scholars and reformers have interpreted and explained the nuances of '*Dharma*', and thus managed to update the doctrines to keep them relevant. This acceptance of differences and the process of periodic reformation have instilled tolerance among Hindus, and they have retained the fundamentals of Dharma during all the invasions, occupation and colonization throughout the ages. This is the foremost reason that the most sincere efforts of Muslim and Christian missionaries to convert Indians have failed. In spite of political and economic domination of Muslims and Christians for centuries, most Indians have not converted to Islam or Christianity, even when they faced differential treatments and imposed hardships.

Chapter XXIV

PHILOSOPHY

Between the seventh and fifth centuries BCE, there was much progress in intellectual life in Greece, China, Israel, and in India. In India, the teachings of Upanishads were crystallized and elaborated by learned scholars, or Sages, who taught established foundations of philosophical schools. At the same time, some philosophers, such as, Sankara and Ramanuja, Buddha and Mahavira, were later regarded as founders of world religions[3].

The Sanskrit term used to translate philosophy is 'Darshana'. Darshana is a derivative of the verb 'Drisha' or 'to see' or 'to realize', and literally means 'realizing truth and reality through reasoning and intuition'. "A Darshana is a spiritual preception, a whole view revealed to the soul sense",[5]. As the foundation of Hinduism, particularly Bramhanism, lies on philosophical discourses of 'Shastras', mainly of Vedas and Upanishads, Indian philosophy has been often found not only overlapping but also forming much of the foundation of Hinduism. Indian philosophy has been often misunderstood in the West as being mainly concerned with the affairs of spirit and after life. However, further study reveals that it is also concerned with developing philosophical paradigms that were grounded in reality. Particularly, the texts of Upanishads debate the value of the real world, as well as the spiritual world. Indian philosophers have mainly discussed the importance of 'Atman" or 'Soul', and the process of soul migration, and established theories through debates, discussions, and contemplation. They also tried to refute the atheistic and skeptical views, which were very powerful and persuasive. Indian philosophy has a place for the discourse of contradictory points of views, and this capability of acceptance and inclusion has been reflected in Hindu religion. Indian philosophy and Hinduism readily accepted and incorporated new and opposing views.

In Indian philosophy, establishing a theory usually followed three stages: 'Purvapakshsa' or explanation of established and often opposite views, '*Khandan*' or refuting of these views, and finally '*Siddhanta*' or establishing one's own view. Development of Indian philosophy can be found to take place in three periods of history. The pre-logical period, spanned from the creation of Vedas and Upanishads to the Christian era, logical period or to the Muslim domination of India or 1000 AD, and then ultra-logical, when the dialectical method of discourses flourished (1100 – 1700), [2].

Indian philosophy has two main schools of thought: Orthodox and Heterodox. In the orthodox view, the principles and premises of the Shastras, or Vedas and Upanishads, particularly the relation between all living souls and the Divine soul or '*Paramatma*', the process of soul transmigration, and the goal of '*Moksha*' or salvation, are taken as absolute and infallible. Six main schools of thought, developed by sages or scholars, followed these points of view: '*Nyaya*', '*Sankhya*', '*Yoga*', "*Vaiseshika*', '*Mimansa*', and '*Vedanta*' or '*Uttar Mimansa*'. The heterodox view, on the other hand, refutes such premises, and is regarded as '*Nastik*' or atheist and skeptical. The three major schools of heterodox view are the Materialism of Charbak, Buddhism of Gautama Buddha, and Jainism of many sages, mainly Mahavira.

The '*Sankhya*' system, developed by Sage Kapila, is perhaps the earliest of all philosophical schools. In this system, '*Prakriti*' or original substance of all living things consists of three classes of abilities called '*Gunas*' or properties: '*Sattwa*' or truth and virtue, '*Raja*' or active and fiery, and '*Tama*' or dullness and inactivity. The '*Nyaya*' system, developed by Sage Gautam, stressed the view that clear thinking was an essential preliminary to salvation. The '*Yoga*' system, initiated by Sage Patanjali, is not to be confused with the Yoga exercises as known in the Western world. In this system, the importance of pure thought and deed, and the practice of non-violence, truthfulness, and self-control are emphasized.

The '*Mimansa*' school, established by Sage Bhadarayana, who composed the '*Bramha Sutra*' or the Threads of Bramha, is in essence the study of Vedas. The Vedic concepts are clarified, interpreted and crystallized into teachings to form a cohesive doctrine. His work has been further interpreted by different scholars to establish various sects and doctrines. The '*Vaisesika*' school stresses that the soul is completely detached from the cosmos, and this concept must be embraced for salvation. According to this doctrine, cosmos is composed of '*anu*' or atoms of five elements: '*Khsiti*' or earth, '*Jala*' or water, '*Pawaka*' or fire, '*Akasha*' or space, and '*Samira*' or wind. Thus this school also dwells in the scientific realm as well,[2]. This doctrine is virtually identical of the Pythagorean point of view of the cosmos, and it is speculated by scholars that these two schools have had some contacts or influence on each other.

A more elaborated interpretation of the Vedas and Upanishads was undertaken by Sage Sankara (c. 850). He established the doctrine of '*Adwaita*' or no-second or Monoism, stressing that the souls of all loving beings are essentially not separate from '*Paramatma*' or Divine soul, a '*Nirakar*' or an impersonal entity. He was also the first to interpret *Bhagawat Gita*, which by his time had become to be regarded as a collection of all vital concepts of Indian philosophical doctrines. He asserted that the three attributes of human life are to be pursued for salvation: '*Sat*' or truth, '*Chit*' or consciousness, and '*Ananda*' or eternal bliss. His work forms the foundation of the '*Jnana Marga*' or The Way of Knowledge for salvation. In essence, Sankara initiated the method of explaining the Vedas and Upanishads through dialectic process, concluding with a generalized statement. His explanations of Shastras are still readily accepted by most philosophers and scholars. He is regarded as the person who reestablished '*Brahmanism*', after the demise of Buddhism during the Muslim rule in India.

A different approach to Sankara's doctrine of '*Jnana Marga*' for salvation was offered by Ramanuja (c. 1137). He stressed the doctrine of '*Bhakti Marga*;' or The Way of Devotion. He also accepted the concepts of Vedas and Upanishads, including Bhagawat Gita, but he rejected the Sankara's view of '*Paramatma*' as impersonal entity. He affirmed that Vishnu was the '*Purusottama*' or the Supreme Person, and can be represented in an idol form. Salvation, he claimed can be attained through '*Bhakti*' or devotion, which according to him was easier to pursue and more practical for the masses. Devotion, he stressed, can be expressed through rituals, such as the chanting and singing of devotional songs, praying and offering, and living an ascetic life. This principle formed the basis of the '*Vaishnavism*' sect, which has been the dominant segment of Hinduism, and became known in the West through the Hare Krishna movement.

Another philosopher, Sage Madhava (1199-1278), further refined the doctrine of '*Bhakti*' or devotion. He also interpreted Vedas and Upanishads, refuted Sankara's doctrine and established the doctrine of

'*Dwaita*' or Duality. In this doctrine, "Vishnu is not only a Deity, he has also incarnated into human form to help his devotees attain salvation",[3]. Some of these incarnations, in the form of Rama and Krishna, are vividly described in the epics Ramayana and Mahabharata. Readings and chanting of these epics are regarded as the most essential rituals of Hinduism, and is still an important unifying factor in India.

Sage Charbaka was the first heterodox philosopher, who refuted the existence of soul, and thus the transmigration of souls as described in Vedas and Upanishads. He preached the importance of physical pleasure through materialism. He and his followers, such as Makkali Goshala and Ajita Keshakambali, opposed all the principles of orthodox philosophers, and claimed that there is no entity beyond a body. However, the orthodox principles prevailed in India, and Charvaka's doctrines are all but forgotten,[3].

Around the fifth century BCE, a form of heterodox philosophy gaining much importance was established by Siddharta, a prince of Shakya tribe, who lived in Kapilavastu, a small kingdom in the foothills of the Himalayas, bordering modern Nepal. He gave up a life of luxury, denounced all worldly possessions, and became an ascetic at the age of twenty-nine. He attained '*Bodhi*' or enlightenment while meditating under a tree near Gaya in Magadha now in Bihar, India, and was called Buddha by his followers.

Buddha preached a middle way between the extreme asceticism of Vedic philosophy and heterodox view of life being only physical. His doctrine later developed into the Buddhist philosophy. "The fundamental truths on which Buddhism is founded are not metaphysical or theological, but rather psychological",[3]. Buddhism accepts the process of transmigration of soul, but stresses that the journey of soul from body to body takes place according to the laws of *Karma*. "Gautama reacted violently against Brahmanism and against the inhuman nature of sacrifices and prohibitions",[1].

Also, Buddhism claims that no body can attain '*Nirvana*'. In Buddhism, Karma or Action is the most important aspect of human life, and much of Buddhist scriptures elaborate the proper actions of man.

According to Buddhism, there are three '*Smaranas*' or refuges of man: '*Buddha*', '*Dhamma*' (Pali for Dharma), and '*Sangha*' or the Assembly of the Elect, later to become the Assembly of '*Bhiksus*' or Monks. After his death, Buddha was deified as God, and formed the first refuge.

'*Dhamma*', the second refuge, consists of actions prescribed for attaining enlightenment. '*Sangha*', the third refuge, consists "...of those of Buddhas followers who, having renounced the household life, devote the whole of their time and their energies to the realization of Nirvana",[5]. These followers were known as '*Bhiksus*' or beggars, as they survived through charity of other people.

Buddhism flourished around the early centuries of Christ, particularly during the reign of Emperors Bimbisara and Ashoka (542-237 BCE). These emperors patronized Buddhism, and built temples, 'Stupas' or mounds, and monasteries for Buddhist monks. Two great universities for the study of Buddhism in Taxila and Nalanda were also established during this time. Buddhism also spread to the South and East of Asia, and Buddhism is still the major religion of this area.

When the Gupta dynasty reigned in India (319-540), Buddhism started to decline in India. Brahmanism was revitalized by Sankara, and after the death of King Harsha, who was the last Buddhist monarch, Buddhism lost the royal patronage. Finally, when the Muslim invasions began in 1100 AD, and when Muslim rulers began destroying Hindu and Buddhist establishments, Buddhism, in essence, ceased to be a major philosophical doctrine in India. Buddhists needed the monasteries to gather and practice their religions, and the Buddhist 'Bikhus' or monks, wearing saffron and saved heads, were easily recognized and became targets for the Muslim oppressors.

Hinduism, being a way of life, survived among its followers. Hindus did not need temples in which to pray, and they could practise any ritual, follow any doctrine of their choosing from an array of principles. Due to their capability of flexibility and inclusiveness, Hindus accepted Buddha as one incarnation of Vishnu, and Buddhism was included in the fold of the ever- expanding realm of Hinduism. Even after centuries of Muslim occupation and European colonization, Hinduism survived in India.

Another philosophy, called Jainism was established in India around the sixth century BCE, which also refuted the doctrines of Vedas and Upanishads. In the eighth century BCE, a scholar named Parsva, who was a prince of Varanasi, renounced all wealth and became a monk. His teachings were not to destroy life, not to lie, not to steal and not to possess anything. His followers, known as *Tirthankars*, spread these values until Mahavira (1199-1278) revitalized them into a coherent form of doctrine, called Jainism. He introduced the practice of chastity and the severest form of non-violence.

Jainism refutes the role of God in the life of a man, and asserts that only the actions of man determine whether a man is to be reborn or is to be dissolved into the absolute,[6]. The other significant principle of Jainism is the strict adherence to non-violence, and prescribes that no living being, even the insects, can be killed. Jain monks can be seen wearing white face masks fearing swallowing insects and killing them. Jains also follow the strict diet of vegetarianism. Unlike Buddhists, the Jains remained mainly in the southern part of India and were isolated from the north by the Vindhyachal Mountain Ranges, thus they were spared from the oppressive practices of the Muslim invaders. Much of Jain texts are preserved in Jain monasteries in the form of manuscripts in Dravidian languages.

Indian philosophy is different from Western philosophy in many aspects. As it seems, Indian philosophies formed the basis of three great world religions. "Classical Indian philosophy included the discussion of *Moksa*, because its chief concern is with salvation or liberation from the human condition.. Much of Indian Philosophy postulates at the very outset the criteria or sources of valid knowledge that each of them proposes to use and relies on them",[3].

Chapter XXV
SANSKRIT

Most historians claim that Sanskrit is the language used by early Aryans. "The creation of Sanskrit was the greatest accomplishment of the Aryan world in India...An immense scientific, religious, philosophical, and dramatic text was developed, a great part of which still exists, but nowadays is often inaccessible, left lying in manuscript form in innumerable badly classified libraries. If rediscovered, they could one day change many of the notions of about the history and civilization of the world, since only Sanskrit literature has developed continuously, without interruption, down to our times",[2].

The origin of Sanskrit is still being debated among scholars. Some claim Sanskrit to be a rectified version of Indo-European or Indo-Germanic Language. Max Muller, the German philosopher and historian, found some remarkable similarities between German and Sanskrit grammars, and he considered there was a common origin for both languages,[4]. However, other scholars dispute the very existence of such a language. "The creation of Sanskrit, the 'refined language' was a prodigious work on a grand scale. Grammarians and semanticists of genius undertook to create a perfect language,...that was to become the language of the entire culture",[2].

Sanskrit alphabet has forty-eight letters, divided into thirteen vowels, and thirty-five consonants. The consonants are arranged according to their pronunciation in five groups of five. Up to four consonants and one vowel can be blended; blending and diphthongs can be used to yield new letters. There are ten tenses of verbs, and the verbs can be used to produce verbal nouns, gerunds and participles. Adjectives and adverbs can be modified to convey subtle nuances. Sanskrit has a rich vocabulary, and new terms can be coined by combining root words and compounding prefixes, suffixes and verb forms. Verbs can cover a wide spread of tense forms, and the wealth of abstract nouns make Sanskrit a useful language to provide technical, philosophical and psychological terms...Such a rich vocabulary often makes it difficult to translate philosophical, technical, cosmological, and other Sanskrit texts into other languages",[2]. These properties make Sanskrit a language suitable for coining new terms, capable of expressing intricate concepts, and a rich language to create literary works.

It was Panini, who is credited with having created the first organized form of Sanskrit grammar around the fourth century BCE. Around second century BCE, Sage Patanjali used Sanskrit to comment on Panini's grammar. Sanskrit became a rigidly structured language mainly used by scholars. "This grammar was then developed by the philosopher Patanjali in the second century BCE, in his 'Mahavashya' or 'Great Commentary'. Later on, toward the seventh century AD., another philosopher, Bhartrihari, regrouped all previous ideas in his 'Vakyapadiya' developing a whole theory of language from the point of view of semantics, psychology and symbolism. It is one of the most remarkable works that ever been written on the nature of the human phenomenon of language",[2].

The masses used a dialect of Sanskrit, called 'Prakrit', and later, 'Pali'. Around 525 BCE, Pali became the court language of Buddhist rulers, such as Bimbisar and Ashoka. Both Buddha and Mahavira's teachings are recorded in Pali dialect. By the fifteenth century, a number of regional languages emerged from Sanskrit. Within a few centuries, all these languages created vast and rich literatures. However, the influence of Sanskrit remains very strong on these languages. Sanskrit remains the language of scholars and poets, and Sanskrit is still used for all religious activities in India.

Sanskrit had been initially used to create religious texts. The first known such works are the Vedas. Vedas, derived from the Sanskrit root word 'Vid' meaning knowledge. There are four Vedas: Rig, Sam, Yajur, and Atharva Vedas. Rig Veda is the first one, and became a standard followed by the creation of other Vedas, during the period of 1500 to 1000 BCE,[2]. Vedas consist of hymns, and they also describe the 'Yajnas', or "...rituals to be performed for purifying one's mind so that they may become fit for receiving the knowledge of God",[5]. Upanishads mainly deal with the questions of how a man is related to God, how God can be realized, and how the knowledge of God, can be attained. There are many Upanishads, but the main ones are: *Isha, Kena, Katha, Prashna, Mundaka, Mandukya, Aitreya, Taittriya, Chhandogya, Brihadaranyaka*, and *Shwetashwatara*. Later religious works in Sanskrit consist of Smritis, created by Sages, such as, Manu and Yagnavalka. They prescribe codes of human conduct, list prohibitions, and allocate special duties to be performed by man in various stages of life or 'Ashrams'.

Two great epics, *Ramayana* and *Mahabharata*, are the next remarkable examples of Sanskrit literature. Ramayana, created by Sage Valmiki, known as '*Adi Kavi*' or the First Poet, describes the character of Rama. To most Hindus, Rama is the perfect personality. Ramayana has been an inspiring source for millions of Indians throughout several centuries, "...there has been no more inspiring symbol of Dharma than the hero of the epic Ramayana, a text that gives expression to both the social and devotional tendencies..."[3]. Ramayana has been translated in practically all the Indian languages, and is still recited all over India. Mahabharata, on the other hand, composed around 900 BCE by Sage Dwaipayan or Vyasa, narrates the conflict between human ambition and duty through a battle between two groups of princes of a ruling dynasty. *Mahabharata* still fascinates Indians, which exemplifies the struggle of human characteristics in metaphoric narration and sets examples of best human behavior and the importance of fulfilling one's duties. One section of Mahabharata consists of '*Bhagawat Gita*', or Songs of the Gods. It clarifies the essential concepts of Dharma, and is regarded as the 'cream of all Vedas'.

Sanskrit has also been used for secular literary works. The first genre of Sanskrit literature is '*Natyashastra*' or the Art of Drama. Bhasa of the second century, Dandin of the seventh century, and Kuntaka of the eleventh are the well known literary figures of this genre. In '*Kavya*' or poetry genre, Ashwaghosa of the first century, Mentha and Kalidasa of the fifth century, are also known for their great literary works. Emperors of Gupta dynasty, particularly Vikramaditya II, patronized poets in their courts. Kalidasa, also called '*Maha Kavi*' or Great Poet, created some of the most memorable works of Sanskrit literature, such as, '*Meghadutam*' in lyric form, '*Kumarsambhavam*' in drama form, and '*Raghuvansham*' in epic form. Kalidasa also created some novels, such as, '*Malvakikagnamirta*', '*Vikramorvasia*' and '*Abhigyansakuntalam*'. These works mainly centre around love, and depict the aspirations of female characters. The heroes in his creations are helpless characters who are victims of supernatural powers,[7]. Some other literary personalities of Sanskrit literature are Bhasa, who is "...regarded as the greatest master of Sanskrit prose"[7], Bhavabhuti, Bhartrihari, the author of "three hundred lyrics", and Bana of Emperor Harsa's court. Sanskrit works continued to be created throughout all centuries, even when the Muslim and British powers ruled over India, and Persian and English respectively were patronized and supported by the rulers.

The use of Sanskrit was not limited to northern India, where the Aryans settled. In the Dravidian south, Sanskrit became the language of scholars and religious leaders. Sanskrit was spread to South and Far East Asia, where Indian cultural and business influence dominated. Even in modern India, Sanskrit is used not only in religious and social rituals, but also "...as a source of modern languages. Sanskrit is able to provide on a larger scale the new technical terms which are continually needed, and which the modern languages cannot supply from their own sources",[1].

After the Muslim rulers invaded and occupied India around 1100 CE, they established Persian as the court language. Even then, Sanskrit remained the language of scholars and poets, and was used in all religious activities. Some great works of literature continued to be created in Sanskrit, although most works, particularly translations of epics and devotional songs were composed in regional languages of India, most of them stemming from Sanskrit. When the British colonized India in the eighteenth century, they tried to stop the teachings of Sanskrit by replacing it with English, as Ram Mohan Roy petitioned and urged by Macaulay. In spite of all their efforts, and even when English became the only language used in higher institutes of education and employment, Sanskrit remained the main language for most social and religious activities. "...brutal Muslim conquest, followed by European colonization, ...left few linguistic traces on Sanskrit, since the prestige of Sanskrit was so great",[2].

Introduction of the printing press in India, mainly to print the Bible in Indian languages to be distributed by Christian missionaries to convert Indians, opened a flood gate of literary works in all regional languages in India. Indian literature is well known and much appreciated throughout the world, and frequently translated into foreign languages. Much credit for this phenomenon goes to Rabindranath Tagore, who created and enriched almost all segments of literature, and was awarded the Nobel Prize for literature for his creation 'Gitanjali' or Homage of Songs. Two songs created by Rabindranath Tagore are the national anthems of India and Bangladesh.

After independence, the Indian government tried to declare Hindi, a language of roughly one third of Indians, as the national language of India, while keeping English as the official language until 1965, when it was to be replaced by Hindi. This move resulted in much agitation and strong resistance all over India, particularly in the South. A strong proposition was made by many Indians, such as, Rajendra Prasrad, the then President of India and an erudite scholar, and Nalini Ranjan Sengupta, the President of Shastra Dharma Prachar Sabha, and an eminent physician, to declare Sanskrit as the national language of India. Rajendra Prasad pointed out, "..for many centuries past, Sanskrit has provided the basis of unity in India...It enjoyed the status of what we might call the national language of India",[6]. In his speech delivered in Sanskrit at the All India Sanskrit Rastrabhasa Conference, Dr. Nalini Ranjan Sengupta, the Charman of Reception Committee asserted, after citing the uniqueness and strengths of Sanskrit, "Every modern regional language in India was a distributory of Sanskrit. Take away Sanskrit from them, and little will be left with them...Sanskrit has been a great unifying force, common reservoir from which all parts of India have equally derived in culture",[6].

Chapter XXVI
SCIENCE & MATHEMATICS

The Sanskrit term for Mathematics is '*Ganita*' or the 'science of calculation' and for Science is '*Vigyan*' or 'significant knowledge'. Growth of
scientific ideas in India can be grouped into five distinct periods. During
the Vedic period, geometry and astronomy were developed for the construction of altars and fire pits. Scholars consider this period to be around
the eighth to fifth centuries BCE[9]. From the fifth century CE, several
great mathematicians and scientists developed mathematics and astronomy, usually patronized by the Gupta and Bardhan rulers. This period is
also known as the first renaissance in India. From the twelfth century to
nineteenth century, under the Turkish and Moghul rule, very few scholars
did foster science and mathematics, and their work was mainly aimed to
find "something unique" for consumption, and their works remained limited to their own social circles,[5]. Lastly, under the British rule, several
Indian scientists ushered in the "modern" era of science and technology,
and gained worldwide recognition. At present, there are several internationally well-known scientists working in facilities for scientific research
in India.

There is evidence of scientific development even during the pre-
Vedic period. The early known civilization in India flourished in the
Indus Valley around 3000 BCE. According to the artifacts and objects
found from archeological discoveries at Mohen-jo-daro and Harappa
there are indications that the inhabitants of these locations were techno-
logically advanced and they possessed skills to construct planned cities
with underground sewage systems and well-fired bricks to withstand the
harsh climate. Evidence has also been found to indicate that they had developed counting and writing capabilities as well. "The people of Indus
Valley had a pictographic script and a decimal numerical system",[6]. Use
of carved stones indicates that they had developed useful tools.

Before the rise of the Aryan civilization, or around 2000 BCE, the
Indus Valley civilization abruptly became extinct. From there on, "...

much of Indian science is to be influenced by the speculative and philosophical mind, to be richer in generalization",[6]. In the West, scientific advancements were made through empirical data and deductive discourses. Unlike the Greek scholars, early scholars of India did not attach their names or dates with their work therefore it is rather difficult to set a precise chronology of scientific advancements and their sources in India. As no record of the process for scientific advancements has been found, it is assumed that in India, an intuitive and speculative process was used, which yielded some useful outcomes. Some of these are in the form of scientific and technological applications, such as, use of spokes in wheels, chariots equipped with harness, and the use of metals, such as, silver, iron, gold and lead in weapons and jewelry are chronicled in the *Vedas*, which were created around 1000 BCE.

Vedas also contain references to astronomical bodies, and a description of the construction of altars with precise geometrical treaties. As the Vedas were more concerned with the spiritual and philosophical concepts, only fragmented information about sciences are included. Of all *Sutras*, seven have survived. *Baudhyana, Apastamba* and *Katyayana Sutras* reveal a wide range of mathematical treaties, including the construction of equivalent squares. A better source of Indian science of that period can be found in well known treaties such as '*Arthashastra*' by Kautilya, '*Samhita*' by Charaka, and *Sulva Sutra* and *Surya Siddhanta* by Aryabhatta.

Hindu mathematicians also dealt with geometry and trigonometry. Similar to the Greeks, they also considerd square as the basic form, but switched to circle around 200 BCE, as stated in '*Surya Pragnapati*'. The Jaina scriptures also describe precise calculations of a circle using the ratio of diameter and circumference as the square root of ten. This also shows that as early as in 400 BCE, scientists in India had the concept of irrational numbers. Jaina texts also include the calculations for the length of arcs and chords of circles, and solutions of quadratic equations. Calculation of '*Vikalpa*' or permutations and combinations was a favorite topic of Jain mathematicians as chronicled in '*Bhagawati Sutra*', (c. 300 BCE). Similarly, Buddhist texts deal with astronomical calculations to explain the structure of the universe as they saw it,[6].

Hindu mathematicians were also very interested in numbers, particularly in large numbers. In the epics *Ramayana* and *Mahabharata*, as well as in *Chandogya Upanishad*, place values of ten up to 53 has been mentioned. "Hindu mathematics is undoubtedly the first intellectual achievement of the subcontinent...It brought alongside the Greek geometrical legacy a powerful method in the form of analysis...The Hindus excelled in attaining perfection of the decimal system, developing the concepts of fractions, negative integers, quadratic equations, complex numbers, and irrational roots",[12].

Kautilya's 'Arthashastra' is a revealing document of Hindu science. He was the Prime Minister of Chandragupta Maurya, who founded the Maurya dynasty and ruled from 321 to 300 BCE. Artha Shastra provides a "... store of information on land and sea communications, agriculture and irrigation, ores and mining, plants and medicine, and especially mechanical contrivances or 'yantras'",[12]. One such device mentioned in Arthashastra is Variyantra, a water spraying device to cool the air, which has been mentioned by poet Kalidasa of that time in *Malavikagnimitra*.

The stone carvings of Maurya Emperors and universities built at that period reveal that in addition to incorporating advanced building techniques, Indians had used a numerical system with 'zero', and had developed a precise calendar system. Under the patronage of the rulers and nobles, the cities of Ujjain, Pataliputra and Mysore became centers of Hindu science. This tradition continued during the Gupta period and beyond.

Mathematics had fascinated the Hindus since the time of the Vedas. The works of Hindu mathematicians, such as, Aryabhatta I (c. 499 CE), Varahamihira (c. 505 CE), Bhaskara I (c. 600 CE), Bramhagupta (c. 628 CE), Mahavira (c. 850 CE), Aryabhatta II (c. 950 CE), Bhaskara II (1114-1185 CE) reveal great discoveries. This tradition has continued to the present time with many Indian mathematicians contributing to new developments in mathematics.

Aryabhatta I wrote the first known mathematical text 'Sulva Sutra'. Sutra literally means 'string' or 'rope', which were used for measurement and construction. Construction workers, such as, masons and carpenters are called 'Sutradhar' or string holders in Sanskrit. During this time, Hindu mathematics was mainly concerned with the geometrical construction of 'Yagna Kunda' or altars for holy fire,[1]. *Baudayana Sutra* also shows the method of calculating the length of 'dwikarni' or diagonals and squaring of a circle, using the value of square root of two as 1.4142156. "To construct fire altars or 'Jagna Vedis', Hindu mathematicians introduced the concept of 'Bija Ganita' or algebra. The irrationality of square root of two was understood in the time of the *Sutras*,[12]. *Sulva Sutra* describes the construction of right angles with ropes, indicating the knowledge of Pythagorean triads. *Sulva Sutra* also describes the construction of perpendiculars, bisectors, rectangles, trapeziums, and isosceles triangles. It also describes a method to construct a circle with an area equal to a given rectangle,[12]. Apasthamba, another mathematician of that time, described a process of converting a triangle into a square.

In the second century, several '*Siddhantas*' or systems were created under the patronage of the rulers of Gupta Dynasty. This period has been called the "Golden Period" of Indian History, when the first renaissance of Hindu culture is said to have taken place. Five Siddhantas are known to have been created at this time: *Paulisha, Surya, Vashista, Paitamaha,* and *Romanka*. Varahamihira, a mathematician in the court of Chandragupta Vikramaditya, has described all five Siddhantas in detail,[6]. *Paulisha Siddhanta* cites the value of Pi to be 3 and 177/1250, which is very precise.

Aryabhatta II's *Surya Siddhanta* is the most significant of treaties of Hindu mathematics. It deals with the calculations of spherical trigonometry and applies the place value of ten,[1]. Bramhagupta, in '*Bramhagupta Siddhanta*' mentions the process of solving linear equations with integral solutions. He presented the general solution for Diophantine solution,[1]. He also contributed a great deal in the area of intermediate analysis and the formation of Pythagorean triads,[12]. The knowledge contained in the *Siddhantas* has been mentioned by the Arab scholar and traveller Al-Beruni.

Bhaskara II described the process of intermediate analysis of solving equations in his '*Siddhanta Siromani*', which is divided into several parts: *Lilavati, Bijaganita, Goladhya, and Grahaganita*. Bijaganita describes a unique solution of Pythagorean Theorem using a practical demonstration by cutting the two squares, which has been described as the "Hindu Solution", as compared to Euclidian deduction. *Lilavati* deals with several topics of Hindu mathematics, such as, solving linear and quadratic equations, arithmetic and geometric progressions, and surds,[1].

In *Grahaganita*, Bhaskara II has described the motion of a planet by dividing the day into a large number of intervals, and comparing the position of the planet at the end of each successive interval, which he termed as "*Tatkalika Gati*" or instantaneous motion. He states that "At the commencement and end of retrograde motion, the apparent motion of the planet vanishes" (translation by Colebrooke). This idea of limit was formulated by Bhaskara II five centuries before Newton and Leibnitz. "Bhaskara conceived the differential calculus and the differential coefficient",[3].

The concept of limit was further dealt with when "Operational difficulties were felt in dealing with the number zero...which lead Bramhagupta to regard zero as an infinitesimal quantity which ultimately reduces to naught",[2]. The process of quadrature of a circle has been described by Aryabhatta II in Verse 17 of *Surya Siddhanta*. "The emphasis Hindu mathematicians placed on the numerals and the principle of notation did, of course, make more easily possible the development of ...the algorithmic process of calculus",[2]. In *Goladhya*, Bhaskara II has explained the trigonometrical formulae in Verses 7, 9, 13, 21 and 22. Just as in verses 57 to 65, he has described the process of integration to find the volume of a sphere using '*ekadhika sutra*' or partial fraction. He has also stated that when 'any number is divided by '*Shunya*' or zero, the result is '*Khacheda*' or 'nearing sky', indicating the concept of infinity.

In '*Ganita Kaumudi*', Narayana has described the process of '*Varasamkalika*' or Summation of series. Nilkantha has further elaborated the method of summation of infinite series in '*Yuktibhasa*'. Summation of trigonometrical series is described in *Tantrasanghita*, but the authorship of this treaty has not been established.

Irrational numbers have been described in *Sulva Sutra* as well. It has led to the irrational value of Pi. Nilkantha has described that "the ratio of the circumference to the diameter can never be expressed as the ratio of two integers" (Translation by Colebrooke)[3]. Well before that, Aryabhatta I has used the value of Pi as the square root of 10 in Verse 40, of '*Bramhasiddhanta*'. Nilkantha in ''*Karma Paddhiti*' has used the value of Pi as 31415926536 divided by 10. In *Lilavati*, Bhaskara II has used the ratio of 31416 and 10000.. Aryabhatta II has described the calculation of the of Pi in Verse 208, that yields the value of 3.1416...,[2].

The concept of '*Shunya*' or nought or space has been prominent in the Vedas. The exact time for the application of zero in the numerical system as a decimal place value by the Hindus is a topic of debate among scholars. The decimal place value system was first explained by Aryabhatta I who left a "permanent impression on the mathematics of later generations –the place value numeration—...his phrase 'from place to place each in ten times the preceding' is an indication that the application of the principle of position was in his mind",[1].

The inclusion of zero in the numerical system was a significant development in mathematics. "With the introduction in the Hindu notation of the tenth numeral, a round goose egg for zero, the modern system of numeration for integers was completed",[1]. With this development, the Hindus introduced the modern system of numeration. "The new numeration, which we generally call the Hindu system, is a new combination of three basic principles, all of ancient origin: a decimal base, a positional notation and a ciphered form for each of ten numerals...it is due to them that the three were first linked to form the modern system of numeration",[1].

Astronomy was a significant area of study among the Hindu scientists. Even in 500 BCE, '*Jyotish Vidya*' or astronomy has been applied to create the Hindu calendar, indicated as '*Samwat*', which is still used in India to set time and date for religious ceremonies. This calendar system, described in '*Vedanga Joytisha*' accurately calculates the position of the moon and twenty seven '*Nakshatras*', or stars, and sets the '*Ayanas*' or date cycles,[12]. Hindu astronomers could precisely calculate the eclipses, and the methods established by them are still used today. Varahamihira had calculated the movements of celestial objects which are recorded in '*Pancha Siddhanta*' (c. 505). Other notable treaties of Hindu Astronomy are '*Bramhasphuta Siddhanta*' by Bramhagupta (c. 628 CE), '*Sisya-dhi-Vidhhyidha*' by Lalla (749 CE), '*Vateswara Siddhanta*' by Vateswara (c. 904 CE), '*Siddhanta Sekhara*' by Sripati (c. 1039 CE), and '*Siddhanta Siromani*, by Bhaskara II (c. 1150 CE).

Science in ancient India also dealt with Physics and Chemistry. In *Kevaddha Sutra*, a theory is described for the formation of '*anu*' or molecule by '*paramanu*' or atoms grouping together. Chemistry, in the form of alchemy, was an integral part of *Tantric* ritual. Nagarjuna has described the "mercurial remedies and the chemical behavour of metals",[12].

In the area of medicine, Hindus developed the Aurveda system. According to the ancient language of Sanskrit, Ayurveda translates to "ayus" meaning life and "veda" meaning knowledge. In other words, Ayurveda translates to Science of Life (Wujastyk, 2003). Ayurveda is more than just treatment of diseases. The philosophy behind Ayurveda is to heal the body by bringing ones mental, physical and spiritual states into harmony. It embraces a holistic approach and stresses "a life style which is designed to prevent illness",[11].

Ayurveda as a practice of medicine was taught in the ancient Universities of Takshashila and Nalanda in India, which are considered as some of the most noted and respected universities of that time. Those universities also taught Economics and Philosophy and were believed to be the birthplace of certain large sects of Hinduism and Buddhism. As a result, Ayurveda was originally rooted in popular culture and took a holistic approach as opposed to a separate form of medicine altogether.

Although documented references to Ayurveda are not available, it is considered that the study dates back to the origin of the Vedas. The growth in popularity for Ayurveda eventually gave rise to the normal mode for the health care system in ancient India and is believed by some to spawn the eventual establishment of modern healthcare practices,[10].

Ayurveda was one of the first practices of medicine to use surgery as a form of treatment. However, that changed during Emperor Ashoka's (304 BC-232 BC) rule in India due to his law to prevent any bloodshed whatsoever. Thus Ayurveda adopted a more medicinal and pharmaceutical approach to treatment and veered away from surgery.

The earliest discovered Ayurvedic text is *Charaka Samhita* written by Charka, *Sushruta Samhita* and *Astanga Samhita* written by Sushruta,[7]. Critical revisions of these texts has been written by the famous Hindu scholar Vāgbhata at the beginning of the seventh century CE. Charaka Samhita, the most significant text, was an etiological one written by Mādhav called *Nidāna*, an anthology of works outlining diseases along with their causes, symptoms and complications. Over centuries thereafter, the texts and literature for Ayurveda have been revised and become more detailed.

In modern times, several Indian scientists and mathematicians have become famous for their contribution to modern science. Sriniwasa Ramanujam (1887-1920) was a mathematical genius who made a substantial contribution in the fields of mathematical analysis, infinite series, and number theories. Prof G. H. Hardy recognized his genius and invited him to go to Cambridge University. In England he became very sick, and once, when Prof. Hardy visited him at Putney, he told Ramanujam that he came in a taxi that had a dull number of 1027. Ramanujam immediately answered that 1027 is a very interesting number as it is the least integer that can expressed in two different ways as the sum of two cubes: $1^3 + 12^3$ and $9^3 + 10^3$.

Chandra Shekhara Venkata Raman (1888-1970) was a physicist who is credited with the discovery of Raman Ray in the spectrum. He received the Nobel Prize for physics in 1930. Prasanta Chandra Mahalanobis (1893-1972) was a statistician who designed the model for plan for growth that the Government of India used to draw up the five-year plans. He also designed tools for surveys and founded the Indian Statistical Institute.

Sir Jagadish Chandra Bose (1858-1937) invented coherer, and used semiconductor junction to detect radio waves in 1900, and this device was used by Marconi to invent radio in 1902. He also contributed in the field of plant sciences. He established the Bose Research Institute for scientific research, which is still functioning. Satyen Bose (1894-1974) was another well-known physicist who established many theories in the area of quantum physics and is famous for discovering Bose-Einstein condensate. He is honored by the naming of the element Boson after him.

Homi Bhaba (1909-1966) is regarded as the architect of India's nuclear and space programs. These areas were further developed by scientists such as, A. P. J. Abdul Kalam (1931) and Raja Ramanna (1925-2004). Dr. Abdul Kalam became the President of India in July 2002.

Chapter XXVII
MUSIC AND DANCE

Similar to most aspects of Indian culture, the first evidence of music can be found in the Vedas. In India, music in all forms is a reflection of its diversity, and focuses on the spiritual and religious lives of the people. Music has played a vital role in India, and has been appreciated throughout the ages. Indian music originally developed from the chanting of Vedic texts, mainly from the Sam Veda. Vedic chants in Sanskrit with its accents and dronish recitation makes a rich foundation for classical music,[2]. As a result, music has remained an integral part of religious and spiritual activity in India, and has been pursued by people of all classes. In the epics *Ramayana* and *Mahabharata*, learning the art of singing and dancing are mentioned as parts of the training of the youth. The most revered text of Hindus is '*Shrimadbhagawat Geeta*', or "The Song of the Lords", signifying the importance of music in Indian lives.

Sage Narada is named as the first musician in Hindu mythology. Music is described to be evolved from the primal sound of "OM" with seven notes: *Shadja, Rishabh, Gandhara, Madhyama, Panchama, Dhaivata*, and *Nishada*,[1]. The first syllables of these basic notes or Sa, Re, Ga, Ma, Pa, Dha, Ni, and Sa, are still used to learn classical music. Indian music can be grouped into three basic forms: classical, devotional and folk. Classical music has a strict foundation of theory and structure, based on '*ragas*' or melodies and '*tala*' or rhythms, but non-classical music is full of harmony and beats. Although Indian classical music has a well established structure, there is an opportunity of individual improvisation and creativity.

Ragas, a derivation of the Sanskrit term '*Rangas*' or color, are usually associated with natural scenes and celestial happenings, and their emotional settings are taken from Hindu mythology. Composition of ragas is fully explained in *Natyashastra*, the first text of Indian music compiled by Sage Bharata around second century BCE. In this text, ragas are described as consisting of a set of melodies, with a rhythmic counterpart.

The six original ragas are *Hindol, Bhairav, Deepak, Megh, Shree* and *Maulkauns*. Other ragas are derived from these ragas. Each raga must have '*swar*' or notes. In raga, there must also be '*thaat*' or '*mela*' or a modal structure, and '*jati*', according to the number of notes used. Most ragas also have particular '*rasas*' or moods, depending on the scene they are developed. There are nine *rasas*: Love (*Shringar*), Humour (*Hasya*), Pathos (*Karuna*), Anger (*Rudra*), Heroism (*Vir*), Terror (*Bhayanaka*), Disgust (*Veebhatsa*), Wonder (*Abdhuta*) and Peace *(Shanta)* .[2].

"Bharat's *Natyashastra* gives significant information about Indian music, various concepts related to it, and musical instruments, and serves as an indispensable link between music during the Vedic period, music in the epics, Panini, Buddhist and Jain works, and the music during the time of Matanga and Sarangadeva",[2]. The next significant text for music is *Brihaddesi*, written in the seventh century, by author Matanga. He describes the ragas in further detail. He describes the five 'pure' or original ragas, and submits a list of '*bhinna*' or altered or improvised ragas. According to him, raga is "...that which is a special dhwani, is bedecked with notes and is colorful or delightful to the minds of the people, is said to be rāga"[1]. *Dhwani* is the Sanskrit term for sound.

By the thirteenth century, author Sarngadeva describes over 264 ragas in his book '*Sangitaratnakara*' which were created by that time. To remove confusion and eliminate overlapping, ragas were reclassified in the thirteenth century based on their ethos rather than characteristics. From there on, Indian classical music was divided into two distinct forms: 'Hindustani' or northern and 'Karnataki' or southern Indian music.

Ragas in the Karnatic music are mainly of two types, the original *melakarta ragas* and the derived or *janya ragas*. *Melakarta* ragas have a formal structure. Each raga consists of seven rhythmic cycles. However, the *janya* ragas have more room for improvisation. Many *janya* ragas have changed their character over time. The current system of Karnataki ragas is mainly the creation of Venkatamakhi in 17th century CE,[2].

'*Tala*', a Sanskrit word meaning claps or rhythm patterns, is based on '*aksara*' or the smallest time unit, and '*matra*' consisting of four aksaras. Each tala can be played in three distinct tempos: '*vilamba*' or slow, '*madhya*' or medium, and '*druta*' or fast. The most common talas are: *Tintala* (or *Trital*), *Tiwara, Ara Chautal, Dipchandi, Jhumra, Dhamar, Ektal, Chautal, Jhaptal, Sitarkhani, Kaharwa, Roopak,* and *Dadra.* "Raga and Tala are both independent bases for composition and improvisation and may be heard as such in a concert",[2].

Music is still taught orally by '*Gurus*' or teachers, and the learning period spans over years. Learning to sing in classical form requires a strict and disciplined structure. Gurus play an important part of all individuals associated with Indian music. Gurus develop distinct traditions of performance and style of presenting based on their locality or '*gharanas*', and their disciples follow these traditions to the letter.

In Hindusthani vocal music, a more structured style called '*Dhrupad*' is the most prominent. It begins with an '*aalap*' section which can be improvised, followed by '*sthyai*', '*antara*', '*sanchari*', and '*abhog*' sections,[1]. After the Islamic influence, the '*Khayal*' or imagination style of vocal music developed which became popular. In this version, there is more room for improvisation and it has less emphasis on words. During the Muslim rule, several genre of vocal music, with more room for improvisation and creativity, were developed. At the same time, a form of music in fast tempo, called '*tarana*', also became popular as well,[1].

Music was much patronized by the Muslim rulers, and they often invited musicians and composers to their courts. Under their tutelage, Hindustani music made great progress. For example, Amir Khusru (1254-1325), a court musician in the court of Alauddin Khilji contributed a great deal to the development of Indian music. He is credited with the creation of several ragas, three of them, *Hemant*, *Prabhat Kali* and *Hem Behag*, are well known. He also developed the music instrument Sitar, a stringed instrument, which is mainly used for rhythm, but lately has become a solo instrument also. Another great musician, Mian Tansen (1506-1509), was invited by Emperor Akbar to be his court musician. Tansen created many famous ragas, such as, *Mian Ki Todi*, *Mian Ki Malhar*, *Mian Ki Sarang*, *Darbari Todi*, and *Darbari Kanada*. He also created over one thousand Dhrupads.

Similarly, Hindu rulers in the South patronized musicians in their courts as well. Teaching of Karnataki music was standardized by Purandara Dasa (1480-1564), who also created several thousand songs, mostly in Kannada language. In the eighteenth century, Muthuswamy Dikshitar (1775-1835) composed over four hundred songs and Kirtanas in Sanskrit, and is credited for the introduction of the use of the violin in Indian music. Thyagaraja (1767-1847) created over one thousand songs in Sanskrit and Telegu, and pioneered the 'Sangati' form of music. He also created two operas in Telegu. The annual Thyagaraja festival, celebrated in his honor, is attended by thousands of music lovers.

Another form of vocal music, called *'thumri'* became popular particularly for the devotional songs during the *Bhakti* movement in northern India. Saint singers, such as Meerabai, Kabir, Tulsidas, Surdas, Kesavdas in north India, Jayadev, Bidyapati, and Ramprasad in Bengal, Thyagaraja, Dikshitar, and Shyama Sastri in south India, created thousands of songs in various regional languages of India A new genre of songs, called *'Bhajans'* or prayers, mainly based on the romantic adventures of Lord Krishna and his lover Radha, two deities of Hindu mythology became a regular form for devotional songs.

Chaitanya Dev in Bengal made the *'Kirtan'* form of devotional songs popular. In this form, Gods' names are repeatedly chanted, and it is usually performed by groups. Bhajans and kirtans are still the two essential forms of devotional music in India. Both Hindu and Muslim mystic singers, *'Bauls'*, and *'Sufis'*, composed and performed songs with deep philosophical and spiritual contents. During the nationalist movement, patriotic songs, such *'Bande Mataram'* by Bankim Chandra Chattopadhya, became a significant source of inspiration to many freedom fighters. Many such songs are still performed in schools, clubs and community organizations all over India.

Due to the influence of Islam in India, *'qawwalis'*, a highly improvised form of vocal music developed in northern India. Qawaalis are composed in Urdu language and are highly improvised. Very often, performers create the song during their performance. Performers of qawaalis were patronized by the nobility, and the tradition is still practised. Very often, Hindu Bhajans and Islamic Qawaalis are performed by the same individual at the same time. *'Gazas'*, another form of qawaalis describing erotic situations but with mystical themes, were initially made popular by Sufi singers, but became popular among the general population in time.

Modern music has been enriched by numerous composers and performers, who have become an essential and integral part of India. No other personality has contributed more than Rabindra Nath Tagore (1862-1941). He composed over three thousand songs, and introduced an original form, called *'Rabindra Sangeet'* fusing classical, devotional, folk and even Western tunes with his own distinct form. His creation is admired by many in the world, and appreciated all over India. Both India and Bangladesh have chosen songs created by him as their national anthems.

Folk music in India originally developed among the tribal groups and manual labor class, such as, farm workers, ferry boat rowers, and mystic singers, adhering to both Hindu and Islam religions. They composed songs describing their daily rituals, feelings and hardships. Many folk songs are based on ceremonial situations, such as birth, death, marriage, and religious activities. Secular songs are performed during functional situations, such as during planting and harvesting crops, ferrying across a river, and weaving cloth. Greeting songs, lullabies, ballads are also abundant. Songs of courtship, particularly describing the pains of separation and unfulfilled love, make a rich source of folk songs,[1].

Instruments used with Indian music consist of melodic, rhythmic and drone instruments. The most ancient melodic instrument is the *'veena'*, which is the instrument held by Saraswati, the Hindu deity of "learning and culture", and Narada, the first musician of Hindu mythology. Some other melodic instruments are *venu or bansuri* or flute, violin, sitar, sarod, sarangi, and shahnai. Sitar, made known to the Western world by Ravi Sankar, is used as a rhythmic and as a solo instrument as well. Most common rhythmic instruments are *tabla, dholak or drums, mridangam, kanjira, and tavil. Tambura and tanpura* are the two most common drone instruments. *Harmonium*, a hand-pumped keyboard device is also used, particularly in Northern India, as a secondary drone instrument. Most tribal and folk songs are sung unaccompanied or just accompanied by drums,[2]. A single string-plucking instrument, *'Ektara'*, literally meaning 'one stringed', is also used by wandering singers. There are numerous other musical instruments used regionally, locally, and individually.

Evidence of dance as an ancient activity has been established with the finding of a five thousand years old bronze statue of a dancing girl belonging to the Indus Valley civilization. In Vedic Ages, dancing became a religious ritual. It was also a means of expression and entertaining activity as well. The first known treaty for dancing, is *'Natyshastra'*, which was compiled by Sage Bharata around 200 BCE. He has described the art of dancing or *'Natyaveda'* as the fifth Veda. *'Natyshastra'* incorporates *'Pathya'* or text from Rig Veda, *'Abhinaya'* or communication with body from Yajur Veda, *'Geet'* or music from Sam Veda, and *'Rasa'* or emotional elements from Atharva Veda,[4].

Examples of dancing are abundant in India. Dancing *'Apsaras'* or court entertainers are carved on the gateway of Sanchi Stupa, a Buddhist relic built in 300 BCE. The frescos of Ajanta and Ellora of the fourth century show dancing figures, and the temples in Khajuraho, built at the time of Hoysala Dynasty in the tenth century show dancers in erotically suggestive poses. In the south, *'Devdasis'* or temple dancers were common in the tenth century,[3].

Hindu mythology has many evidences of dancing, beginning with *'Nataraja'*, the dancing form of Shiva. Bigger than life-size dancing Natarajas in 81 poses are prominently displayed on the Badami temple built in 578 CE. In the epics Ramayana and Mahabharata, and the Puranas, dancers belonging to Gandharva (modern Kandhahar?) and Kinnari tribes are prominently described. Dancing has been an integral part of Indian social, cultural and religious lives throughout the centuries.

Classical dances in India can be originally grouped into three styles: *Bharat Natyam, Kathak* and *Odissi*. However, in time, regional dancing styles have also developed, such as, Bharat Natyam in Tamil Nadu, *Kathakali* in Kerala, *Odissi* in Orissa, *Kathak* in Uttar Pradesh, *Manipuri* in Manipur, and *Kuchipudi* in Andhra Pradesh,[4]. All these dances have their own fundamental and rigid movements and poses, but they also leave room for improvisation and creativity. Similar to classical music, classical dances are also taught by 'Gurus' under strict and structured conditions. The individual and distinct styles of Gurus have yielded *'gharanas'*, and the learners follow these styles of performance faithfully and diligently.

Bharat Natyam is based on movements in space mostly in straight lines and triangles. The body of the dancer is divided into three parts for interpretive poses and movements: *'Anga, Pratanga, and Upanga'*. The body is set into graceful bends or *'bhangas'* and movements called *'Anga Lakshanas'* or body postures. In the classical form, the dancer focuses on hand movements and *'mudras'* or poses to interpret *'rasas'*. The torso is used as a unit, and the legs form the stances. In interpretive form, expresses emotions with facial and body gestures, and usually interprets a poem or narration of the Puranas or Epics.

Kathakali interprets stories of Puranas with hand signs, and through natural, rhythmic and graceful gestures. This style of dancing is based on both the Aryan and Dravidian styles, and is composed of three arts forms: *'Abhinaya'* or acting, *'Nritya'* or dancing, and *'Geeta'* or music. Dancers also use bright colors on their costumes representing and interpreting moods of mythical characters and incidents.

Kathak literally means 'story telling'. In this dance form, the dancers narrate mythological and historical occurrences through movements, mimics, and music. It originated among temple dancers, but has evolved with the influence of Persian culture. Rhythmic legwork and spinning movements with straight legs, and facial expressions are the important features of Kathak style. With individual creativity, Gurus develop distinct styles or '*Gharanas*', named after their localities, such as, Lucknow, Gwalior, Benaras, and Jaipur. Originally this dance form was performed mainly by '*Tawaifs*' or professional female entertainers, and thus often used to carry a stigma.

Manipuri dance originated in the Eastern most part of India. It consists of delicate, graceful and lyrical movements. The dancers adorn themselves with colorful costumes and sparkling ornaments. This dance form originated as a religious activity, but has evolved as a social activity without losing its sacred connotation. Performers do not interact with the audience, but concentrate on communicating with the Lord. The style has remained ritualistic in nature, and is enriched with '*Bhakti*' or devotional sentiments.

Kuchpudi dance originated around 1500 AD at Kuchelapuri in Andhra Pradesh. Siddhapa, an ascetic, redefined and reorganized this dance style from a strictly religious activity to a social and cultural activity for all devotees of Lord Krishna. He incorporated movement from folk dances of the area, freeing it from strict classical structure. This dance form uses mimes, movements and facial gestures to express feelings.

Odissi dance is the classical dance form of Orissa. It is highly stylized and has remained mostly in its original form with an unbroken tradition. It originated in the Jagannath Temple in Puri as a devotional dance performed by '*Devdasis*' or temple dancers. In strict ritualistic form, this dance progresses in predetermined stages, changing postures, rhythms and facial expressions. Often, the body is gracefully bent in '*tribhanga*' or in three places: the head, the bust and the torso. Gradually this dance spread into general population in '*Nartaki*' tradition through the patronage of the local rulers.

Similar to his music, Rabindranath Tagore has fused classical, folk and even Western dance forms with his own creative genius to introduce a unique dancing style, presently called '*Rabindra Nritya*'. He has incorporated his dance and music style into several dance dramas which are performed all over India.

In addition to these major styles, there are numerous regional and folk dance forms in India. Such as, *Bhangra* in Punjab, *Gharba* in Gujarat, and *Jhaunaach* in Bengal, just to name a few. Practically every locality and every linguistic, tribal and social group has distinct dance forms for religious, social, and cultural festivities. In modern form, dances are still evolving with the influence of Western culture, just as the Eastern and Middle Eastern cultures have influenced Indian dances in the past.

Chapter XXVIII

ART AND ARCHITECTURE

Evidence of art and architecture in India can be found even before the Vedic times. Artifacts such as coins, seals and sculptures have been found in Mohen-jo-Daro and Harappa, where an ancient civilization thrived around 2000 BCE. Some such findings are "The "lord of the beasts', the naked girl with a dancing figure with one leg lifted diagonally across the other, the sacred bull, the short masculine torso, the 'tree of life', an innumerable types of monkeys, females, cattle and carts modeled in terracotta",[4].

Coins found on these sites indicate that the use of metals for sculptures was well known. "The most striking works of Indus cities are small steatite seals carved with copper bruin, coated with alkali, and baked to glaze the surface",[2]. These coins bear images of various animals, such as, bull, elephant, bison, and crocodile. These scattered samples represent unbroken and flourishing artistic activity. The sculptures are mostly made of stone or wood, whereas paintings are works done on palm leaf or cloth. It is assumed that many such paintings have perished in the harsh climatic conditions of India. Only some paintings on the wall of caves and large terracotta sculptures have survived. The cities were planned and architecturally well designed. "At its cultural hub were the planned cities of Mohen-jo-Daro and Harappa, which boasted straight roads and affluent residences with bathrooms served by a sewage system",[3].

Samples of art created during the rise of the Aryan civilization have also been found mainly in the Ganges Basin. Arts found in the form of sculpture have been found in Rajghir that dates back to around the sixth century BCE. Other samples have been found in the palaces in Kaushambi, which were built around the third century BCE. Hand modeled jewels, figures of dancers, and various deities such as Vishnu and Shiva have been found in the ancient cities of Chandraketugarh and Patliputra, believed to have been created around 200 BCE. Moreover, some such art forms are found in South East Asia, where Indian culture had spread during that time.

Maurya rulers erected pillars and plaques with inscriptions, perhaps being influenced by the Greek culture. Many tall pillars show that art was well advanced during this period. Inscriptions and edicts on rocks, plaques and pillars, decorated with huge sculptures made of polished sandstones were erected by Ashoka (272-232 BCE), and are regarded as showcases of advanced art form with a Buddhist flavor. "These fully polished pillars were carved of tan-coloured sandstone from a single quarry at Chunar",[2]. One of Ashoka's pillars has four lion heads with 'chakras' or chariot wheels mounted beneath it. Only three of these lion heads is visible from any point. Independent India has chosen the image of three lion heads from Ashoka's pillar as the national seal, and the wheel adorns the centre of the India's flag. Ashoka's monuments and pillars are found in other places in South Asia, such as Burma and Thailand, where both Hindu and Buddhist religions spread as well. Many Buddhist rulers also built monasteries for Buddhist monks and buildings to house Buddhist scholars using advanced architectural styles.

Buddhist rulers also built 'stupas' or mounds "...to contain and honor the body relics of Buddha",[2]. For the next few centuries, art and architecture developed around religious centers as monuments and monasteries or 'Viharas', such as in Bharut, Mathura, Bodh Gaya in the north, and in Amaravati and in the Krista Delta region in the south. Monuments and monasteries in Amaravati and Mathura are decorated with elaborate carvings, with railings and gateways, constructed with pillars and spires. As time went on, the style and design of these constructions grew in sophistication and artistry. Most these monuments are adorned with the scenes depicting the life of Buddha, themes of Buddhist legend, and are surrounded with dancing figures. Between 120 BCE and 400 CE, over a thousand viharas were built,[3].

Many temples were also built in caves. Caves offered many advantages: they were cool and dry, most caves were away from localities and thus perfect places for meditation and contemplation, and most importantly, they sheltered these temples from the harsh climate,[2]. In a pictorial style, the walls in the caves at Ajanta and Ellora show advanced style of art form. These temples have survived the ravages of time, but not vandals.

An exceptional style of art and architecture developed in the 'Gandhar' (modern Kandahar ?) area that straddles the natural route for India from the Middle East and Middle Asia, from where most of the invaders and settlers, such as, Persians, Greeks, Kushans, Arabs, Huns and Mongols originated. The invaders and settlers influenced the existing Indian style by developing the Gandhar Art form. The famous Buddha statues at Bamiyan in Afghanistan demolished by the Talibans were created in this style. This style can be found in Japan, Korea, and China as well.

Under the rule of Kushans, temples for Hindu deities Vishnu and Shiva were built in style that was continued in the construction of palaces and temples during the Gupta dynasty. Kushan rulers "...indeed had an eye for all that is beautiful and were connoisseurs of art",[2]. Buddhist shrines continued to be built during the Gupta dynasty, alongside with the construction of Hindu temples, in places in Bihar, Orissa and Bengal. These buildings used wood, brick, and stone to fill structures built with stone, terracotta and bronze. Around this time, courtyards and buildings built with different patterns were used to build Nalanda University,[4].

Although the Hindu style of art and architecture has already been used to build temples in the second century, it was revived in temples built in the Gupta dynasty. "In Hindu architecture, the beauty and complexity of geometrical design, whose underlying principle is harmony",[3]. When the Gupta dynasty ended, rulers of the Pala dynasty in Bengal continued the tradition. These temples contained statues of Hindu deities, such as, Visnu and Siva, and of the Mother Goddess Durga or Kali and usually had a concentric space around these statues where worshippers could pray and meditate. They did not have courtyards or gates. These temples also had crowning towers and hanging bells. The walls used to be decorated with miniature statues depicting scenes from the epics or Puranas. These type of Hindu temples were also built in Mathura, Udaigiri, and Gujarat.

In Rajasthan in the western India, Hindu temples used to have large squat towers with high spires, and open pillared balconies. Temples in Khajuraho in central India had carved statues of dancers in erotic poses. The profusion of beautiful but nude female dancing figures in temples have often been misunderstood by historians. However, "Indian religious art is not concerned with 'carnal' beauty as such but with 'higher spirituality",[3]. Temples in Bhuvaneshwar, Puri and Konarak in Orissa were built around 1000 to 1230 CE. The Jagannath temple in Puri and the Sun temple in Konarak are famous for their magnificently carved sculptures and beautiful paintings on the wall. Unlike the temples of western and northern India, most of these temples survived the ravages of Muslim rulers.

Similarly, the temples in southern India, separated by the Vindhyachal Mountain Ranges, were also spared from the deliberate and systematic destruction carried out by the Muslim rulers, although they did occupy the northern strip of this section in the thirteenth century. Most temples in this region were built by the Pallav, Chalukya and Chola rulers during the seventh and eighth centuries, as "Creating a stone temple to enshrine a divine image was an expensive proposition, and temple-building was largely undertaken by royalty, nobility and highly placed ecclesiasts",[2]. These temples consist of towers surrounding a central cell, composed of several storied pavilions decorated with relief sculptures, roofless corridors, pillars and surrounding walls.

The temples in Mahavallipuram, built around 760 CE by the Pallav rulers best illustrate the Hindu art form. The temple at Kailasnatha and the carved temple at Elephanta are composed of large sculptures, including the famous 'trimurti' or three headed form of Siva. This 'trimurti' image has been selected as the symbol of India. The temple at Tanjore built during the Chola dynasty around the eleventh and twelfth century, is nearly 200 feet high and surrounded with an eighty ton domed capstone, and has exquisite bronze statues.

Temples also built during these centuries by the rulers of Chalukya dynasty in Ambarnath and Bombay (Mumbai), show the influence of the style used in the north and have elaborate squat exteriors, and the interiors have columns with horizontal molding. Similar influence of the north can be found in the temples built by the Hoysala rulers in the twelfth and thirteenth centuries. After this time, Muslim domination in India was virtually complete, and building of Hindu temples ceased.

From the year 1193 to the eighteenth century, the Muslim invaders ravaged India. "From the tenth century, the northern plains of India were convulsed by the raids of the neighbouring Turks and Afghans, who were lured by the legendary wealth of the temples...",[3]. When Turkish rule in India was established around 1206 CE, the rulers began building mosques, palaces, tombs, forts and mausoleums, where art and architecture flourished. Many mosques were built on the site of demolished Hindu temples. The mosques, following the strict edicts of Islam, contained no portraits, statues or pictures, but were decorated with intricate geometrical patterns and flowery designs adorning the walls and minarets. Most mosques followed a standardized form as the Jami Masjid, "...consisting of a large open rectangular court surrounded by arcades or colonnades on all four sides...In the centre of the back wall of the sanctuary, and in the inner side, stood the '*mihrab*',...The call to worship was chanted by a '*muezzin*' from a gallery near the top of a minaret",[1].

Most craftsmen and builders of these mosques were Hindus, and the presence of the Hindu architectural style is evident,[1]. During the thirteenth century, the Turkish rulers built tombs and palaces and mosques. The famous Kutub Minar was built by the Turkish ruler Kutub-uddineibak. The mosque in Ajmer has arches decorated with Arabic lettering. Next, the Tughlaq rulers built the capital city of Old Delhi, the first Muslim city built in India, and remained the capital of the Muslim occupied region of India. In 1911, the British built the new section in Delhi as their new capital city. Since independence, New Delhi has remained the capital of India.

From this period on, several cities with forts, palaces, '*baghs*' or gardens with fountains, and tombs were built by successive Turkish rulers in places such as, Siri, Tughlaqabad, Firozabad, and Jahanpannah. In Bengal and Gujarat, the mosques also contained defensive walls and strategically placed minarets to reinforce Delhi rule, as the provincial governors of these remote places had a tendency to rebel and become independent. Until the beginning of the Moghul dynasty in 1526, mosques were built away from Delhi, in places such as, in Jaunpur, Varanasi, Khairpur and Ahmedabad. These localities also played the role of outposts and an excuse to erect military settlements to "protect" the mosques,[1].

From 1526, when Babur began his rule to, 1707, when Aurangzeb died, most constructions show more distinct a style of art and architecture. Babur built the now infamous Babri masjid and two more mosques in Panipat and Rohilkhand. These mosques show a blend of Indian and Persian architecture. Emperors Akbar (1556-1605) and Shah Jahan (1625-1658) built mostly palaces and forts, but Aurangzeb (1658-1707) built mostly mosques.

Akbar was an enlightened ruler, who loved the arts, music and literature. "It was the third monarch, Akbar, who not only stabilized and expanded the empire, but also left his inedible impact on the architecture and painting in India",[2]. He built forts and palaces with lavish gardens in Delhi, Agra, Lahore, Faterpur Sikri, and Allahabad. He also built tombs, but he is better known for his beautiful palaces and forts. Even his forts included gardens and palaces for his Hindu and Muslim queens, and he used Hindu craftsmen more readily. His most famous palace is in Fatehpur Sikri, which has the great 'Buland Darwaja" or the High Gate, and the two palaces Diwan-i-Khas and Diwan-i-Am.

Akbar's son Jahanghir (1605-1628) also built mosques, palaces, and gardens, such as, Moti Masjid or pearl mosque in Lahore, and palaces in Fatehpur, Srinagar, and Udaipur. These palaces are known for their beauty, luxury and decorations. "The Mughal passion for gardens was developed by Jahanghir and Nur Jahan who explored both the terraced hillside garden and the riverfront garden",[2].

Jahanghir's son Shah Jahan is famous for building the Taj Mahal, a mausoleum for his wife Mumtaj. "The Taj is one of the greatest buildings of the world, and has inspired every serious critic who has seen it to express his admiration",[1]. The great dome, slender minarets, huge doorway, rectangular center and galleries are built with dazzling white marble decorated with precious stone inlays in delicate patterns. The surrounding garden adds more beauty and a river reflects the entire building which is breathtaking. He built palaces in Agra, Ajmer, Delhi and Lahore, one of them, Mumtaz Mahal, named after his wife. Mosques, such as, Jami Masjid and the mosque of Wazir Khan were also built by him. All these buildings are built of marble or sand-stone, and are decorated with inlays. This art is commonly known as the Moghul art form.

In the south, the independent Muslim rulers of Bijapur built over sixteen hundred mosques and several palaces. The mosques include ornamental minarets, great domes and cornices. The great dome of Bijapur is one of the largest free standing domes, and is regarded as an engineering marvel. Also in the South, the ruler of Vijayanagar also built some beautiful Hindu temples. Many temples in south India resemble a 'Ratha' or chariot. In the north, Hindu Rajput rulers of smaller kingdoms in northwestern India also built palaces, forts and temples. All this glory came to an end when Moghul emperor Aurangzeb conquered Bijapur in 1686. Aurangzeb, son of Shah Jahan, was an ascetic and devout Muslim ruler. He built many mosques all over India, often deliberately destroying Hindu temples. He never built any palaces or gardens.

It is ironic that Muslim rulers were great admirers of fine living, who appreciated and patronized art, literature and music, and left a legacy of great architecture, but were often brutal and violent when they imprisoned their fathers and assassinated their brothers to gain power. Most of them also treated their non-Muslim subjects harshly. Muslim rulers did build magnificent palaces and tombs, but they were only interested in their pleasure and glory. The rest of the population remained in harsh living conditions, devoid of infrastructure, and the cities grew in an unplanned and haphazard way. Many Muslim rulers plundered and destroyed temples, and some built mosques on those very sites.

The British continued the tradition of building magnificent buildings, memorials and parks blending Hindu, Muslim and European architectural styles. In building huge and lavish administrative buildings, Viceroy Wessely responded to his critics by saying that "India ought to 'be ruled from a palace, not from a country house; with ideas of a Prince, not those of a retail-dealer in muslins and indigo'",[3]. The British also built large railway stations, but mostly ignored the historical significance of existing buildings. "Undoubtedly the long occupation of the chief cities of India by British army officers with little sympathy for historical architecture led to clumsy and sometimes barbarous treatment of certain buildings, such as those royal palaces which lay inside forts",[1].

PART IX

SUMMARY AND CONCLUSION

Chapter XXIX
SUMMARY AND CONCLUSION

As stated in the previous chapters, India is supposed to have "Unity in Diversity", as if the diverse features of India do merge to form a common basis, which might be considered to be the foundation for nationhood. Metaphorically, it is similar to a "Melting Pot", which has been often used to describe the situation in the United States of America. Canada on the other hand, has been described as "The Vertical Mosaic", as it strives to preserve the unique aspects of different cultures to foster a multicultural society. Shasi Tharoor, a former Undersecretary of United Nations, claims that the description for India should be, "Diversity in Diversity". He elaborates this notion of India as a '*Thali*' or a lunch or dinner plate, where all the food items are presented separately on the same dish. Considering all the information obtained here, it can be concluded that none of these metaphors are completely appropriate for India.

It has been previously established that in spite of all the diversities, Indian society has the Vedic life style, as stated in the '*Shastras*' as the common element, which can be ascribed as holding the society together in spite of all of its diversities. In addition, these diversities make the society more interesting, colourful and enjoyable. Therefore, a more suitable description would be the '*Pushpamala*' or a "garland of flowers" held together by a unifying thread. Whatever description or metaphor is used, India still remains an enigma.

As history shows, major sections of India have been politically united from time to time under a dominating ruler, but have easily disintegrated into smaller entities, ready for foreign invasions. Although these invaders and other settlers did infuse their cultures, but instead of being totally replaced or dominated, the Vedic life style with its ideals of spirituality and religiosity, has not only survived but been reinforced throughout India's history by spiritual leaders and social reformers.

In the same manner, modernity has also been absorbed without losing India's original base of spirituality and religiosity. According to Edward

Luce, bureau chief of Financial Post, India is emerging as an important economic and political force on the world stage while maintaining an intensely religious, spiritual, and in some ways, superstitious society, unusual by the standards of many countries. He further states in his book *In Spite of The Gods*, that in India, the modern lifestyle is just another layer on the country's ancient palimpsest. It is simply adding modernity to what it already has. He also claims that finally the cult of sacrifice and self-denial is losing relevance in a country where commercial values are spreading among all people. They no longer associate religion with poverty or celibacy. Materialism is gaining a hold in India.

It must be noted that secularism in India is not simply a separation of 'Place of worship and State', or disassociation with all religious matters of the government, but also an introduction of laws and regulations to eliminate social injustices which has been practised in public life in the name of religion. Many in India consider such steps as interference and intrusion by the government in their religious beliefs, and meddling with their long- held social customs and traditions.

This situation poses several questions: If the Vedic life style is totally eliminated, would there be any thread of unity remaining in India to hold the nation together? Could India grow as a nation without the solid foundation of Vedic culture? What lies in the future for India: an economically prosperous multicultural nation growing in harmony, similar to Switzerland, or a nation breaking down along religious and ethnic lines, similar to Yugoslavia? The very survival of India as a democratic nation is at stake. It is worth considering that Switzerland is not only multilingual with three major European languages, but unlike India, it is composed of one religion, one race, and one ethnic group. On the other hand, Pakistan broke disintegrated into two separate states on the basis of cultural and linguistic lines, in spite of having a common religion.

In addition to this overwhelming diversity and pluralism, India faces other challenges as well. Corruption among government employees and politicians is rampant. As practically all aspects of Indian's life are regulated by strict permits and licenses, government workers have the opportunity to demand bribes. Bribery is usually the norm in most transactions with the officials.

Politicization of development hinders many worthwhile projects and stifles others. Unnecessary delays and procrastinated actions, added with sloth, stop worthwhile projects. Many politicians fan communal hatred and regional acrimony to achieve short-term political gains. Strikes are often called on the basis of political ideology just to show the power of a self proclaimed leader or a political party. Different forms of political agitations, such as, *'bundh'* or closing down, *'hartal'* or general strike, *'gherao'* or swarming and *'pathrodh'* or closing down roads, have become a regular part of Indians' lives. Long processions of slogan chanting 'dissenters', usually consisting of reluctant participants, who have been bribed, bullied or extorted by political activists, close down traffic and businesses, causing immense hardship on working people.

Most interestingly, in West Bengal, strikes are often called by the governing Communist Party (Marxist), or by labor unions affiliated with them. Often, they strike protesting another strike, imposing loss of income of the poor daily workers and small businesses, the very 'proletariat' the Communist Party claims to represent. Strikes called by a governing party are unheard of in most other democracies.

In spite of a growing middle class, poverty among the majority is still daunting. India grows by over four million people every year. Over three hundred millions live under poverty lines, and there are over six hundred thousand villages deemed to be extremely poor. Unemployment among the undereducated youth is alarmingly high. As India has mostly developed in the service sector, industries have not been developing as much. Private industries in India have employed only one million out of over one billion people. Only thirty million workers pay any income taxes in India.

Elementary education has been practically ignored, as only a fraction of the total budget is allocated to public education, and even then, the major part goes to fund higher education. Public schools are horribly run, depriving millions for proper basic education. In public schools in Bihar, over one third of the teachers are absent in any given day. Similarly, on most days, there is no activity in 50% of all public schools, for an array of reasons, but mostly due to truant teachers. More than half of all schools do not have electricity. Most schools do not have toilets.

Child labor flourishes in spite of the passage of a law banning child labor. Over half of all children do not complete eight years of education, and only one out of ten children attend college. It has been estimated that over forty million children are working as laborers using a loophole in the law where children can work in small scale or cottage industries. Children also work as domestic servants, and as servers and cleaners in restaurants and in sweat shops.

India, often described as the "largest democracy", has the challenges and opportunities of a democratic society as well. In the election of 2009, over eight thousand candidates from three hundred and sixty-nine political parties contested for 543 seats. In a country, where over seventy-seven percent of the population earns less than twenty dollars per day, and over three hundred million live below poverty lines, more than half of all elected members of the parliament are *"crorepatis"* or possessing over one *crore* or ten million rupees, approximately two hundred thousand dollars, an exorbitant sum for most Indians. Also to be noted, 155 of all parliamentarians have criminal records. The cabinet has seventy-eight members, many of them are in obsolete or redundant ministries to represent demographic and caste based quotas and to pacify regional and linguistic groups.

India needs to take drastic and decisive actions to counter all the challenges it faces, but the parliamentary system promotes indecision, factionalism and delay. Indian political parties do not have well-defined principles, other than some "motherhood" types of catchy and rhetorical phrases, such as, socialism, secularism, and Gandhianism. Leaders switch parties and alliances, and blatantly participate in horse-trading, raising the pathetic specter of 'musical chairs'. Most politicians are morally corrupt and unqualified to legislate, but are skilled in underhanded political maneuvers.

Indian society, similar to most societies of the world, faces the realities of globalization, climate change, and terrorism. Indian businesses cannot remain subsidized and protected by tariffs, as they have been protected all along. They have to compete and deliver goods to survive. Some economists such as Vandana Shiva see globalization as a major threat to India's economy. She warns that "...globalization destroys economic sovereignty and democracy. It therefore creates terrorism and violence. It carries the seeds of its own destruction". However, it must be noted that globalization is already here and is inevitable, and it must be addressed by all economies.

Climate change poses food shortages, in addition to other problems. One degree rise in average temperature reduces the output of wheat production by five to eight tons per acre. The rivers of India are extremely polluted, and many are dying. Water from rivers is used for many daily chores, such as, bathing, washing clothes, religious activities, and for cooking. In addition, rivers are the main means of irrigation and transportation. Rivers also contributes to land formation with highly fertile silt, helping yield more food grains. As more and more trees are cut for fire wood, forests are diminishing, resulting in less rainfall, dying rivers and other ecological disasters.

India is also blessed with some opportunities. With a large consumer base, and a growing middle class, consumer goods have a ready market. Basic consumer products are being bought by the young, who are restless and ambitious and demand more in life. Over 50% of India's population is under the age of 25. Allured by this growing market, foreign investments have risen, creating more employment. Belatedly, the government has invested resources to improve infrastructure and that has brought in a boom in construction industry. With investigative reporting vigorously undertaken by a vigilant and free press, and an independent judiciary system, corruption has decreased remarkably.

With an English speaking and young work force, India has the potential to have a booming economy. Better schools, although mostly the private schools, have produced a generation of ready and able group of workers. In 1947, there were only 17 universities, as compared to 350 in 2008. Twelve percent of all between the age of 18 and 25 attend colleges. This pool of highly-trained workers is the main force behind the progress in India. Most young educated people do not share the life-style of frugality, sacrifice and non-materialism that most of the older generation did.

New industries, such as, software engineering, biotechnical and pharmaceuticals, financial management and alternate energy, in addition of information technology, have been initiated by young Indian entrepreneurs. India seems to have entered the post industrial economy. Indian engineers and scientists have been a vital force in the growth of economies of Europe and North America for a long time. Some of these entrepreneurs, such as, Mukesh and Anil Ambani of Reliance industries, Nandan Nilekani of Infosys, Azim Premji of Wipro, Ratan Tata of Tata Industries and producers of Nano cars, Lakshmi Narayan Mittal, Narayana Murthy, Sunil Bharti Mittal, Kumar Mangalam Birla, Anand Mahindra, and Vijay Mallya, have created multinational businesses and become billionaires.

In some ways, India's diversity has also worked as an advantage. Edward Luce claims that India has embraced full democracy before it had a sizable middle class and or majority literacy because it has such diversity, where every group seeks to get involved in the political process to get ahead. Without a nation wide unity, no party or group has been able to produce an absolute dictator. Freedom of speech and a free press with independent judicial system has provided means to express anger and discontent, without initiating nationwide insurgencies. Except the situation in Kashmir which has support from foreign sources, all other insurgencies have been regional, and have failed to destroy India's stability.

India's economy is said to be growing in three main sectors: Information technology, Communication, and Entertainment or ICE. In the National Stock Exchange, ICE industries have grown from only 2% in 1998 to 34% by 2001. Taking advantage of the boom in Information Technology and Biotechnical research, and growth in nuclear and space technology, Indians are more often filling jobs for multinational businesses. Indians are reading MRI's and X-ray images for American clinics, designing management systems for European businesses, and providing actuarial and finance management services for British companies. India is also offering medical procedures for North American and European patients, formally called 'health tourism'. Consumer goods produced by Indian manufacturing enterprises are exported to the Far and Middle Eastern countries.

In the past, the struggle for cultural survival of India was against the domination of foreign cultures. Indians managed to take refuge in their social network and religious customs, and ignored the turmoil in the political and administrative structure. This process is neither possible nor desirable in modern times, as the instant communication system and easy dissemination of ideas through television and the internet are reaching into every remote corner of India, if not to every individual. These realities pose new challenges to its life-style. India cannot remain isolated as it has been throughout history, and must adapt to these realities to survive and prosper. The question is that can it withstand the internal struggle that has invariably begun to find the limitations of changes and a suitable pace for them? Necessities of life have changed the communal life style of the past, and even the social norms and mores are undergoing significant changes, straining the social structure.

These developments are more fundamental and far reaching. Economist and author Gurucharan Das claims that these changes hold a potential to transform India into an innovative, energetic economy of the twenty-first century. Edward Luce, agrees with such an optimistic view, and adds that if carried out sequentially, further liberalization with the elimination of red tape, and with good infrastructure, a literate workforce, sustainable environment, and establishment of law and order, would lead to higher growth and bring greater benefits. He suggests that all these measures are not only necessary to make progress, but essential just to protect India's liberal democracy.

Even considering the dismal record of future predictions, three possible future scenarios can be predicted. First one is optimistic: India will manage to improve its infrastructure and continue to stimulate creativity and innovation to improve economy. With more investment in education and social programs, the middle class will grow further and the gulf between the rich and poor will diminish, resulting in social harmony. Tolerance and inclusiveness will lessen communal and regional feelings, and democratic tradition will strengthen national unity. The centuries- old Vedic values will coexist with the pragmatist and practical initiatives necessary to be taken to meet the challenges of globalization and climate changes. Opportunity presented by the technological revolution will unleash entrepreneurship, and the government policies will adapt to this reality.

The pessimistic scenario is that the narrow and short- term goals of political and communal leaders, both in and outside the government, will resist changes and India will miss out the opportunities presented by technological revolution and globalization. Once again, India will revert back to an economically and an intellectually closed society. Tariffs and control through licences and permits, added to official corruption will destroy most individual's creative aspirations and initiatives. As most of Indian industry is in the service sector, global recession and competition will reduce economic growth. Facing the acute shortage of commodities and resources, social unrest will grow, resulting in communal riots, ethnic strife, and regional conflicts. India will be unable to remain politically united, and once again it will splinter into smaller and vulnerable regions.

The most probable scenario is perhaps a combination of both predictions. Somehow, in spite of all the weaknesses and drawbacks, Indians will achieve successes in some areas, and still survive and muddle through all setbacks. In the tradition of accepting hardships as a result of their own actions or 'Karmaphala', people will slap their foreheads, and suffer through; continuously blaming their fate. The shortsighted leaders will keep on leading a resigned and fatalistic crowd. Some successes and improvements will be cited as major breakthroughs, and people will rejoice. Through all other failures and missteps, Indians will manage to show their surviving and coping skills, and live in a somewhat peaceful and harmonious society, punctuated by local communal conflicts and regional insurgencies.

India as a nation, society and community will prevail and make progress only if it remains true to the Vedic values, such as, tolerance, justice, inclusiveness, celebrating diversity, quest for knowledge, and spiritual superiority, in a traditional society, as it has been throughout its history. In other words, India's past is the future. Also, India must not abandon the feelings of worldliness and pursuit of material happiness, and accept changes needed to survive and make progress in this changing world. If not, as Vijay Kelker, one of India's most famous economists has written in *India's Growth on a Turnpike*, that "The 21st century is India's to lose".

Bengali poet Rabindranath Tagore has expressed what India should strive for in his poem '*Prarthana*' or Prayer, which was first published in *Bangadarshan* in the Bengali month of Baisakh, 1308, or in 1896:

Where the mind is without fear and the head is held high;
Where knowledge is free;
Where the world has not been broken up into fragments by narrow domestic walls;
Where the words come out from the depth of truth;
Where tireless striving stretches its arms towards perfection;
Where the clear stream of reason has not lost its way into the desert sand of dead habit;
Where the mind is lead forward by Thee into ever-widening thought and action...
Into that heaven of freedom, my Father, let my country awake.

CHAPTER REFERENCES

Chapter I-Introduction

1. Durant, W., *The Story of Civilization, Our Oriental Heritage*, New York: Simon and Schuster, 1935,
2. Kishwar, M., *Who am I, Living Identities vs, Acquired Ones*, Manushi, May-June 1996,
3. Luden, D., *India and South Asia*, Oxford: One Land Publications, 2002
4. Marius, R., *A Short Guide to Writing About History*, New York: Harper Collins College Publications, 1995,
5. McMillan, M., *The Uses and Abuses of History*, Toronto: Vikings Canada, 2008,
6. Sachau, E., *Al Beruni's India*, (trans. *Kitab fi tahqiq ma li'l-hind*), New Delhi: Low Price Publications, 1993.
7. Tammita-Delgoda, S., ., *India*, Cambridge: Cambridge University Press, 2006,
8. Tharoor, S., *The Elephant, the Tiger, and the Cell Phone*, New York: Arcade Publishing, 2007,

Chapter II National Identity of India

1. Aloysius, G., *Nationalism without a Nation in India*, Delhi: Oxford University Press, 1997,
2. Durant, W. and Durant, A., *The lessons of History*, Toronto: Vikings Canada, 2008,
3. Embree, A.T., (Ed.), *Sources of Indian Tradition*, New York: Columbia University Press, 1958,
4. Gellner, E., *Nation and Nationalism*, Ithaca: Cornell University Press, 1983,
5. Government of India, "*National Portal of India*", http://www.india.gov.in, 2008,
6. Grover, B, *A New Look at Modern Indian History*, Delhi: Chand Publishing, 1998,

7. Kundra, D., and Kundra, S., *History of India*, Delhi: Navdeep Publications, 1993),

8. Lewis, C., and Short, C., *A Latin Dictionary*, Oxford: Clarendon Press, 1879,

9. Ludden, D., *India and South Asia: A short History*, Oxford: One World, 2002,

10. McMillan, M., *The Uses and Abuses of History*, Toronto: Vikings Canada, 2008,

11. Robb, P., *A History of India*, New York: Palgrave, 2002,

12. Smith, V.A., *The Oxford History of India*, Oxford: Oxford University Press, 1982,

13. Spears, P., *India, A Modern History*, Ann Arbor: The University of Michigan Press, 1972,

14. Tammita-Delgoda, S., *India*, Cambridge: Cambridge University Press, 2006,

15. Tharoor, S., *The Elephant, the Tiger, and the Cell Phone*, New York: Arcade Publishing, 2007,

16. Walsh, J., A Brief History of India, New York: Facts on File Inc., 2006,

17 Wiener, P., *The Dictionary of the History of Ideas*, New York: Charles Scribner's Sons, 1973-1974.

Chapter III India's Heritage-Vedic Lifestyle

1. Derritt, D., "Social and Political Thought and Institutions", Bhasam, A. (Ed.) *A Cultural History of India*, Oxford: Clarendon Press, 1975,,

2. Embree, A.T., (Ed.), *Sources of Indian Tradition*, New York: Columbia University Press, 1958,

3. Kulke, H., and Rothermund, D., *A History of India*, London: Routledge, 2004,

4. Kundra, D., and Kundra, S., *History of India*, Delhi: Navdeep Publications, 1993,

5. Keay, J., *India, A History*, New Delhi: Harper Collins Publishers, 2000,

6. Tammita-Delgoda, S., *India*, Cambridge: Cambridge University Press, 2006,

7. Vohra, R., *The Making of India*, London: M.E. Sharpe, 2001,

Chapter IV India's Physical Features

1. Basham, A., *A Cultural History of India*, Oxford: Clarendon Press, 1975,
2. Government of India, *Geological Survey of India*, (http://www.gsi.gov.in/page2.htm)
3. Keay, J., *India, A History*, New Delhi: Harper Collins Publishers, 2000,
4. Sarkar, R., "*Jivan Nrivignan*" (In Bengali), *Biological Anthropology*, Calcutta: Knowledge House, 2007,
5. Spears, P., *India, A Modern History*, Ann Arbor: The University of Michigan Press, 1972,
6. Vohra, R., *The Making of India*, London: M.E. Sharpe, 2001,
7. Wolpert, S., *A New History of India*, Oxford: Oxford University Press, 2009.

Chapter V Historical Periods and Sources

1. Basham, A., *A Cultural History of India*, Oxford: Clarendon Press, 1975,
2. Deheja, V., *Indian Art*, London: Phaidon Press Limited, 2000,
3. Keay, J., *India, A History*, New Delhi: Harper Collins Publishers, 2000,
4. Kulke, H., and Rothermund, D., *A History of India*, London: Routledge, 2004,
5. Kundra, D., and Kundra, S., *History of India*, Delhi: Navdeep Publications, 1993,
6. Majumdar, R.C., *Ancient India*, New Delhi: Motilal Banarasidas, 1994,
7. Mitter, P., *Indian Art*, Oxford: Oxford University Press, 2001,
8. Mittal, S.C., *India Distorted*, New Delhi: M.D. Publishers Pvt. Ltd., 1998,
9. Sachau, E., *Al Beruni's India*, (trans. *Kitab fi tahqiq ma li'l-hind*), New Delhi: Low Price Publications, 1993.
10. Spears, P., *India, A Modern History*, Ann Arbor: The University of Michigan Press, 1972,
11. Wolpert, S., *A New History of India*, Oxford: Oxford University Press, 2009.

Chapter VI Ancient Civilizations

1. Danielou, A., *A Brief History of India*, Paris: Fayard, 2003,
2. Keay, J., *India, A History*, New Delhi: Harper Collins Publishers, 2000,
3. Kulke, H., and Rothermund, D., *A History of India*, London: Routledge, 2004),
4. Kundra, D., and Kundra, S., *History of India*, Delhi: Navdeep Publications, 1993),
5. Majumdar, R.C., *Ancient India*, New Delhi: Motilal Banarasidas, 1994,
6. Spears, P., *India, A Modern History*, Ann Arbor: The University of Michigan Press, 1972,
7. Tammita-Delgoda, S., ., *India*, Cambridge: Cambridge University Press, 2006,
8. Wolpert, S., *A New History of India*, Oxford: Oxford University Press, 2009.

Ch VII:Invasions, Migrations and Settlements

1. Danielou, A., *A Brief History of India*, Paris: Fayard, 2003,
2. Kulke, H., and Rothermund, D., *A History of India*, London: Routledge, 2004),
3. Sarkar, R., "*Jivan Nrivignan*" (In Bengali), *Biological Anthropology*, Calcutta: Knowledge House, 2007,
4. Smith, V.A., *The Oxford History of India*, Oxford: Oxford University Press, 1982,
5. Tammita-Delgoda, S., *India*, Cambridge: Cambridge University Press, 2006

Chapter VIII Early Kingdoms and Dynasties

1. Keay, J., *India, A History*, New Delhi: Harper Collins Publishers, 2000,
2. Kulke, H., and Rothermund, D., *A History of India*, London: Routledge, 2004),
3. Tammita-Delgoda, S., ., *India*, Cambridge: Cambridge University Press, 2006,

Chapter IX Small Kingdoms

1. Basham, A., *A Cultural History of India*, Oxford: Clarendon Press,

1975,
2. Danielou, A., *A Brief History of India*, Paris: Fayard, 2003,
3. Kulke, H., and Rothermund, D., *A History of India*, London: Routledge, 2004),
4. Smith, V.A., *The Oxford History of India*, Oxford: Oxford University Press, 1982,
5. Wolpert, S., *A New History of India*, Oxford: Oxford University Press, 2009.

Chapter X Turkish Incursions
1. Asher, C., and Talbot, C., *India before Europe*,Cambridge: Cambridge University Press, 2006,
2. Danielou, A., *A Brief History of India*, Paris: Fayard, 2003,
3. Keay, J., *India, A History*, New Delhi: Harper Collins Publishers, 2000,
4. Kulke, H., and Rothermund, D., *A History of India*, London: Routledge, 2004,
5. Wolpert, S., *A New History of India*, Oxford: Oxford University Press, 2009.

Chapter XI Moghul Occupation
1. Asher, C., and Talbot, C., *India before Europe*, Cambridge: Cambridge University Press, 2006,
2. Keay, J., *India, A History*, New Delhi: Harper Collins Publishers, 2000,
3. Kulke, H., and Rothermund, D., *A History of India*, London: Routledge, 2004),
4. Wolpert, S., *A New History of India*, Oxford: Oxford University Press, 2009

Chapter XII British Colonization
1. Keay, J., *India, A History*, New Delhi: Harper Collins Publishers, 2000,
2. Metcalf, B, and Metcalf, T., *A Concise History of India*, Cambridge: Cambridge University Press, 2002,
3. Spears, P., *India, A Modern History*, Ann Arbor: The University of Michigan Press, 1972,
4. Tammita-Delgoda, S., ., *India*, Cambridge: Cambridge University

Press, 2006,
5. Wolpert, S., *A New History of India*, Oxford: Oxford University Press, 2009

Chapter XIII Maratha Resurgence
1. Danielou, A., *A Brief History of India*, Paris: Fayard, 2003,
2. Kulke, H., and Rothermund, D., *A History of India*, London: Routledge, 2004),
3. Wolpert, S., *A New History of India*, Oxford: Oxford University Press, 2009.

Chapter XIV Sikh Resistance
1. Asher, C., and Talbot, C., *India before Europe*, Cambridge: Cambridge University Press, 2006,
2. Danielou, A., *A Brief History of India*, Paris: Fayard, 2003,
3. James, L., *Raj. The Making and Unmaking of British India*, London: Little Brown and Company, 1997,
4. Tammita-Delgoda, S., ., *India*, Cambridge: Cambridge University Press, 2006

Chapter XV Revolts and Rebellion
1. Danielou, A., *A Brief History of India*, Paris: Fayard, 2003,
2. Keay, J., *India, A History*, New Delhi: Harper Collins Publishers, 2000,
3. Tammita-Delgoda, S., ., *India*, Cambridge: Cambridge University Press, 2006,

Chapter XVI Renaissance and Reformation
1. Danielou, A., *A Brief History of India*, Paris: Fayard, 2003,
2. Ludden, D., *India and South Asia*, Oxford: One Land Publications, 2002,
3. Sengupta, N.R., *Our Founder*, Calcutta: Shastra Dharma Prachar Sabha, 2002,

Chapter XVII Rise of Nationalism
1. Danielou, A., *A Brief History of India*, Paris: Fayard, 2003,
2. Metcalf, B, and Metcalf, T., *A Concise History of India*, Cambridge: Cambridge University Press, 2002,

3. Vohra, R., *The Making of India*, London: M.E. Sharpe, 2001,

Chapter XVIII Struggle for 'Swaraj' or Self-Rule
1. Danielou, A., *A Brief History of India*, Paris: Fayard, 2003,
2. Ludden, D., *India and South Asia*, Oxford: One Land Publications, 2002,
3. Tammita-Delgoda, S., ., *India*, Cambridge: Cambridge University Press, 2006,
4. Vohra, R., *The Making of India*, London: M.E. Sharpe, 2001.

Chapter XIX Mass Movement
1. Azad, A.K., *India Wins Freedom*, Madras, Orient Longman, 1988,
2. Hay, N., *Sources of Indian Tradition*, New York: Columbia University Press, 1964,
3. Vohra, R., *The Making of India*, London: M.E. Sharpe, 2001.

Chapter XX Partition and Independence
1. Guha, R., *India After Gandhi*, New York: Harper Collins, 2007,
2. Danielou, A., *A Brief History of India*, Paris: Fayard, 2003,
3. Vohra, R., *The Making of India*, London: M.E. Sharpe, 2001.

Chapter XXI Nehru-Gandhi "Dynasty"
1. Guha, R., *India After Gandhi*, New York: Harper Collins, 2007,
2. Metcalf, B, and Metcalf, T., *A Concise History of India*, Cambridge: Cambridge University Press, 2002,
3. Tammita-Delgoda, S., ., *India*, Cambridge: Cambridge University Press, 2006
4. Vohra, R., *The Making of India*, London: M.E. Sharpe, 2001.

Chapter XXII Rise of Regionalism and Terrorism
1. Guha, R., *India After Gandhi*, New York: Harper Collins, 2007,
2. Metcalf, B, and Metcalf, T., *A Concise History of India*, Cambridge: Cambridge University Press, 2002,
3. Vohra, R., *The Making of India*, London: M.E. Sharpe, 2001,

Chapter XXIII Dharma: A Way of Life
1. Basham, A., *A Cultural History of India*, Oxford: Clarendon Press, 1975,

2. Danielou, A., *A Brief History of India*, Paris: Fayard, 2003,
3. Duneja, P., *The Holy Geeta*, Delhi: Govindnand Hasanand, 1998,
4. Embree, A.T., (Ed.), *Sources of Indian Tradition*, New York: Columbia University Press, 1958,
5. Gauthier, F., *Arise Again, O India*, New Delhi: Har Anand Publishers, 2002,
6. Robb, P., *A History of India*, New York: Palgrave, 2002,
7. Radhakrishnan, S., *The Hindu View of Life*, New York: Harper Collins, 1998,
8. Radhakrishnan, S., "Hinduism", *A Cultural History of India*, Basham, A. (Ed.), Oxford: Clarendon Press, 1975,
9. Sengupta, N. R., *Hinduism is the Only Dharma, Why?*, Calcutta: Shastra Dharma Prachar Sabha, 1938,
10. Sengupta, N.R., *Our Founder*, Calcutta: Shastra Dharma Prachar Sabha, 2002,
11. Tharoor, S., *The Elephant, the Tiger, and the Cell Phone*, New York: Arcade Publishing, 2007.

Chapter XXIV Philosophy

1. Danielou, A., *A Brief History of India*, Paris: Fayard, 2003,
2. Das Gupta, S., "Philosophy", Basham, A (Ed.)., *A Cultural History of India*, Oxford: Clarendon Press, 1975,
3. Embree, A.T., (Ed.), *Sources of Indian Tradition*, New York: Columbia University Press, 1958,
4. Radhakrishnan, S., "Hinduism", *A Cultural History of India*, Basham, A. (Ed.), Oxford: Clarendon Press, 1975,
5. Sangharakshita, B, "Buddhism", Basham, A (Ed.)., *A Cultural History of India*, Oxford: Clarendon Press, 1975,
6. Upadhye, A., "Jainism", Basham, A (Ed.)., *A Cultural History of India*, Oxford: 2007,

Chapter XXV Sanskrit: Language and Literature

1. Burrow, T., "Ancient and Modern Languages", Bhasam, A. (Ed.) *A Cultural History of India*, Oxford: Clarendon Press, 1975,
2. Danielou, A., *A Brief History of India*, Paris: Fayard, 2003,
3. Embree, A.T., (Ed.), *Sources of Indian Tradition*, New York: Columbia University Press, 1958,
4. Muller, F. M., *Sanskrit Grammar for Beginners*, New York, Hip-

pocrene Books Inc., 1870.

5. Nirvedananda, S., *Hinduism at a Glance*, Calcutta: Ramkrishna Mission, 1944,

6. Sengupta, N.R., Speech delivered at All India Sanskrit Rastrabhasa Conference, 1958,

7. Warder, A.K., "Classical Literature", Bhasam, A. (Ed.) *A Cultural History of India*, Oxford: Clarendon Press, 1975.

Chapter XXVI Science, Mathematics and Medicine

1. Boyer, C., *A History of Mathematics*, New York: John Wiley and Sons, 1968,

2. Boyer, C., *The History of the Calculus*, New York: Dover Publications, 1949,

3. Cantor, M., *Die Vorlesungen Uber die Geschichte der Mathematik*, Leibzig: B. G. Teubner, 1900-1908,

4. Colebrooke, H., *Algebra with Arithmetic and Mensuration, Bhaskara and Bramhagupta*, London: John Murray, 1817,

5. Gopal, S., "Social Set-Up of Science and Technology in Moghul India", *Indian Journal of History of Science*, Vol. 4, May and November 1969, New Delhi: National Institutes of Sciences of India, 1969.

6. Mason, S., *A History of the Sciences*, New York: Collier Books, 1956),

7. Rhymer, H., *Ayurveda: The Gentle Health System*, New York: Sterling Publishing Company, 1994,

8. Sastri, K., (Ed.), *Aryabhatiya with Bhasya and Nilkantha*, Trivendrun: Trivendrum Sanskrit Series, No. 101, 1930-1931,

9. Sraswathi, T., "Development of Mathematical Ideas in India", ", *Indian Journal of History of Science*, Vol. 4, May and November 1969, New Delhi: National Institutes of Sciences of India, 1969.

10. Svoboda, R., *Ayurveda for Women*, Rochester, Vermont: Healing Arts Press, 2000,

11. Whitehouse, T., *Student British Medical Journal*, Vol. 21, London: BMJ Publishing Group, January 2006,

12. Winter, J., "Sciense", Bhasam, A. (Ed.), *A Cultural History of India*, Oxford: Clarendon Press, 1975,

13. Wujastyk, D., *The Roots of Ayurveda*, London: Penguin Books, 2003.

Chapter XXVII Music and Dance
1. Bhatnagar, N., *Evolution of Indian Classical Music*, Jaipur: Publication Scheme, 1997,
2. Jairajbhoy, N., "Music", *A Cultural History of India*, Basham, A. (Ed.), Oxford: Clarendon Press, 1975,
3. Kundra, D., and Kundra, S., *History of India*, Delhi: Navdeep Publications, 1993,
4. Vatsayam, K., *Indian Classical Dance*, New Delhi: Government of India, Ministry of Information and Broadcasting, 2007.

Chapter XXVIII Arts and Architecture
1. Briggs, M.S., "Muslim Architecture in India", Bhasam, A. (Ed.) *A Cultural History of India*, Oxford: Clarendon Press, 1975,
2. Deheja, V., *Indian Art*, London: Phaidon Press Limited, 2000,
3. Mitter, P., *Indian Art*, Oxford: Oxford University Press, 2001,
4. Ransom, P., "Early Art and Architecture", Bhasam, A. (Ed.) *A Cultural History of India*, Oxford: Clarendon Press, 1975,

REFERENCES:

Aloysius, G., *Nationalism without a Nation in India*, Delhi: Oxford University Press, 1997,

Asher, C., and Talbot, C., *India before Europe*, Cambridge: Cambridge University Press, 2006,

Basham, A., *A Cultural History of India*, Oxford: Clarendon Press, 1975,

Bhatnagar, N., *Evolution of Indian Classical Music*, Jaipur: Publication Scheme, 1997,

Boyer, C., *A History of Mathematics*, New York: John Wiley and Sons, 1968,

Boyer, C., *The History of the Calculus*, New York: Dover Publications, 1949,

Briggs, M.S., "Muslim Architecture in India", Bhasam, A. (Ed.) *A Cultural History of India*, Oxford: Clarendon Press, 1975,

Burrow, T., "Ancient and Modern Languages", Bhasam, A. (Ed.) *A Cultural History of India*, Oxford: Clarendon Press, 1975,

Cantor, M., *Die Vorlesungen Uber die Geschichte der Mathematik*, Leibzig: B. G. Teubner, 1900-1908,

Colebrooke, H., *Algebra with Arithmetic and Mensuration, Bhaskara and Bramhagupta*, London: John Murray, 1817,

Das, Gurucharan, *India Unbound*, New Delhi: Penguin Books India, 2000,

Danielou, A., *A Brief History of India*, Paris: Fayard, 2003,

Deheja, V., *Indian Art*, London: Phaidon Press Limited, 2000,

Derritt, D., "Social and Political Thought and Institutions", Bhasam, A. (Ed.) *A Cultural History of India*, Oxford: Clarendon Press, 1975,

Duneja, P., *The Holy Geeta*, Delhi:Govindnand Hasanand, 1998,

Durant, W., *The Story of Civilization, Our Oriental Heritage,* New York: Simon and Schuster, 1935,

Durant, W. and Durant, A., *The lessons of History*, Toronto: Vikings Canada, 2008,

Embree, A.T., (Ed.), *Sources of Indian Tradition, Part I*, New York: Columbia University Press, 1958,

Gauthier, F., *Arise Again, O India*, New Delhi: Har Anand Publishers, 2002,

Gopal, S., "Social Set-Up of Science and Technology in Moghul India", *Indian Journal of History of Science*, Vol. 4, May and November 1969, New Delhi: National Institutes of Sciences of India, 1969.

Government of India, *"National Portal of India"*, http://www.india.gov.in, 2008,

Grover, B, *A New Look at Modern Indian History*, Delhi: Chand Publishing, 1988,

Guha, R., *India After Gandhi*, New York: Harper Collins, 2007,

Hay, N., *Sources of Indian Tradition, Part II*, New York: Columbia University Press, 1964,

Jairajbhoy, N., "Music", *A Cultural History of India*, Basham, A. (Ed.), Oxford: Clarendon Press, 1975,

James, L., Raj. *The Making and Unmaking of British India*, London: Little Brown and Company, 1997,

Keay, J., *India, A History*, New Delhi: Harper Collins Publishers, 2000,

Kishwar, M., *Who am I, Living Identities vs, Acquired Ones*, Manushi, May-June 1996,

Kulke, H., and Rothermund, D., *A History of India*, London: Routledge, 2004),

Kundra, D., and Kundra, S., *History of India*, Delhi: Navdeep Publications, 1993)

Lewis, C., and Short, C., *A Latin Dictionary*, Oxford: Clarendon Press, 1879,

Ludden, D., *India and South Asia*, Oxford: One Land Publications, 2002,

Majumdar, R.C., *Ancient India*, New Delhi: Motilal Banarasidas, 1994,

Marius, R., *A Short Guide to Writing About History*, New York: Harper Collins College Publications, 1995,

McMillan, M., *The Uses and Abuses of History*, Toronto: Vikings Canada, 2008,

Metcalf, B, and Metcalf, T., *A Concise History of India*, Cambridge: Cambridge University Press, 2002,

Mitter, P., *Indian Art*, Oxford: Oxford University Press, 2001,

Mittal, S.C., *India Distorted*, New Delhi: M.D. Publications Pvt. Ltd., 1998,

Radhakrishnan, S., *The Hindu View of Life*, New York: Harper Collins,

1998,

Radhakrishnan, S., "Hinduism", Basham, A. (Ed.), *A Cultural History of India*, Oxford: Clarendon Press, 1975,

Ransom, P., "Early Art and Architecture", Bhasam, A. (Ed.) *A Cultural History of India*, Oxford: Clarendon Press, 1975,

Robb, P., *A History of India*, New York: Palgrave, 2002,

Rhymer, H., *Ayurveda: The Gentle Health System*, New York: Sterling Publishing Company, 1994,

Sastri, K., (Ed.), *Aryabhatiya with Bhasya and Nilkantha*, Trivendrun: TrivendrumSanskrit Series, No. 101, 1930-1931,

Sraswathi, T., "Development of Mathematical Ideas in India", ", *Indian Journal of History of Science*, Vol. 4, May and November 1969, New Delhi: National Institutes of Sciences of India, 1969.

Sachau, E., *Al Beruni's India*, (trans. *Kitab fi tahqiq ma li'l-hind*) , New Delhi: Low Price Publications, 1993,

Sarkar, R., "*Jivan Nrivignan*" (In Bengali), *Biological Anthropology*, Calcutta: Knowledge House, 2007,

Sengupta, N.R., "Our National Language", Speech delivered in Sanskrit at All India Sanskrit Rastrabhasa Conference, 1958.

Sengupta, N.R., *Our Founder*, Calcutta: Shastra Dharma Prachar Sabha, 2002,

Sengupta, N. R., *Hinduism is the Only Dharma, Why?*, Calcutta: Shastra Dharma Prachar Sabha, 1938,

Shiva, V., *India Divided*, Toronto: Publishers' Group Canada, 2005,

Smith, A., *Ethnic Origins of Nations*, London: Basil Blackwell, 1986,

Smith, V.A., *The Oxford History of India*, Oxford: Oxford University Press, 1982,

Spears, P., *India, A Modern History*, Ann Arbor: The University of Michigan Press, 1972,

Svoboda, R., *Ayurveda for Women*, Rochester, Vermont: Healing Arts Press, 2000,

Tammita-Delgoda, S., ., *India*, Cambridge: Cambridge University Press, 2006,

Tharoor, S., *The Elephant, the Tiger, and the Cell Phone*, New York: Arcade Publishing, 2007,

Upadhye, A., "Jainism", Basham, A (Ed.)., *A Cultural History of India*, Oxford: 2007,

Vatsayam, K., *Indian Classical Dance*, New Delhi: Government of India,

Ministry of Information and Broadcasting, 2007,

Vohra, R., *The Making of India*, London: M.E. Sharpe, 2001,

Warder, A.K., "Classical Literature", Bhasam, A. (Ed.) *A Cultural History of India*, Oxford: Clarendon Press, 1975,

Walsh, J., *A Brief History of India*, New York: Facts on File Inc., 2006,

Whitehouse, T., *Student British Medical Journal*, Vol. 21, London: BMJ Publishing Group, January 2006.

Wiener, P., *The Dictionary of the History of Ideas*, New York: Charles Scribner's Sons, 1973-1974.

Winter, J., "Science", Bhasam, A. (Ed.), *A Cultural History of India*, Oxford: Clarendon Press, 1975.

Wolpert, S., *A New History of India*, Oxford: Oxford University Press, 2009.

Wood, M., *India*, New York: Random House Ltd., 2007,

Wujastyk, D., *The Roots of Ayurveda*, London: Penguin Books, 2003.

THE FRONT COVER

The cover page displays a '*Chakra*' or a wheel in Sanskrit. The word *Chakra* is derived from the Sanskrit root words '*chruhu*' meaning movement and '*kruhu*' meaning to do. *Chakra* has played an important and vital role throughout the development of Indian culture, all the way from the Vedic era to the present time.

'*Chakra*' is repeatedly featured in '*Dharma*'. Life revolves in a '*Chakra*' of birth-death-rebirth until Moksha is achieved. The universe evolves in '*Chakra*' formation of creation-preservation-detsruction. Stages of happiness and sorrow move in '*Chakra*' formation, moving one stage to another.

According to *Rig Veda* (Verse 164), *Chakra* as a weapon was created by the combined energy of Bramha, Vishnu, and Mahesh, the three main manifestations of '*Paramatma*' or the Supreme Soul. Vishnu and Krishna, the two main deities of Hindu mythology, hold the *Chakra*, and have used it to perform divine functions. Verse 20 of chapter 2 of *Chandika Purana 'Durgasaptashati'*, states that both Vishnu and Krishna created another *Chakra* from their own and gave it to the female deity Durga to fight the demons.

In *Vaman Purana*, verse 82.23 describes that the *Chakra* represents '*Kalchakra*' or the cycle of time. It consists of twelve spokes, representing twelve months. In the epic *Mahabharata*, a formation of warriors during battle is described as '*Chakravyuh*'. In this formation, warriors form seven concentric circles rotating in unison. Avimayu, son of Arjun, the hero of the epic, was killed in battle trapped in this formation.

'*Chakra*' as wheels with spokes was also used in chariots, which were the main means of transportation of the early Aryans. Many Hindu temples were later built designed as chariots with huge wheels, the most famous one being the Temple of Konarak. Emperor Ashoka (273-272 BCE), depicted '*Chakra*' as '*Dharmachakra*' or the 'Wheel of Dharma'. The most prominent '*Chakras*' are inscribed on the Ashoka Pillar and the Lion Capital of Sarnath, both erected by Ashoka. These *Chakras* have twenty-four spokes, representing the teachings of Buddha.

'*Chakra*' adorns the centre of the national flag of independent India. It is blue colored and has twenty four spokes. Dr. Sarvapalli Radhakrishnan, the second President of India and an erudite scholar and philosopher, asserts that "this *Chakra* denotes constant motion and the dynamism of peaceful change" that represents the constant progress India is making.

LaVergne, TN USA
16 September 2010
197198LV00004B/11/P